Genocide in the Congo (Zaire)

D1602868

(Photo Credit: Anonymous author. Put on the internet by Ben Salumu)

Ugandan soldiers, wearing American-made uniforms and boots, after stripping naked a Congolese girl and beating her, are getting ready to rape her. Each one of her arms and legs is held by a soldier while another one cuts her pubic hair. The American and European governments are responsible for this. They support Uganda, Rwanda and Burundi's invasion, occupation of the Congo, and neither condemn these countries for these crimes against humanity and against the Congolese, nor demand that they immediately leave the Congolese territory.

WHERE IS AMERICA? WHERE IS EUROPE? WHERE ARE THE DEFENDERS OF HUMAN RIGHTS, HUMAN DECENCY? 1.7 MILLION CONGOLESE ARE KILLED ALREADY. HOW MANY MORE NEED TO DIE?

Genocide in the Congo (Zaire)

In the Name of Bill Clinton, and of the Paris Club, and of the Mining Conglomerates, So It Is!

Yaa-Lengi M. Ngemi

Writers Club Press

San Jose New York Lincoln Shanghai

Genocide in the Congo (Zaire)
In the Name of Bill Clinton, and of the Paris Club, and of the Mining
Conglomerates, So It Is!

Writers Club Press
an imprint of iUniverse.com, Inc.

For information address:
iUniverse.com, Inc.
620 North 48th Street, Suite 201
Lincoln, NE 68504-3467
www.iuniverse.com

The *Frontispiece* picture was smuggled out of the Congo and published
anonymously on the internet at www.africa2000.com/uganda/butchery.jpg

ISBN: 0-595-13938-8

Printed in the United States of America

Dedication

To the innocent Congolese women raped and butchered, tortured, debased, and buried alive; To the innocent Congolese children tortured, killed, and the babies ripped from their mothers' embrace and wombs; To the innocent Congolese elders, the handicapped, and the disabled massacred and humiliated; And to the Congolese men, innocent from the aggressors' internal proclivities to co-genocide.

May your suffering and dying impel us to swear to never be invaded again, by building an ever powerful and united Congo.

Contents

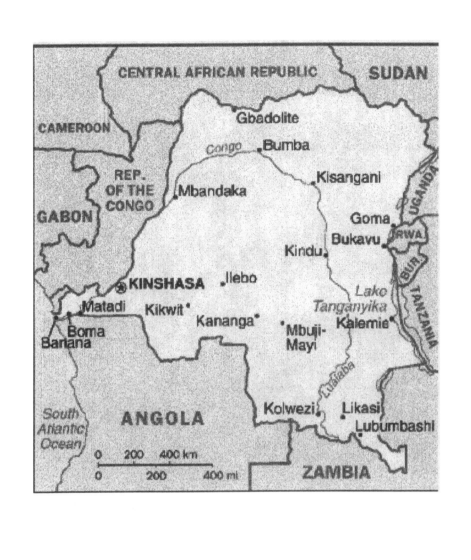

Prologue

HOUSTON, Texas (USA) June 8, 2000 (Reuters)-"Rockets lit the sky over the **American** city of **Houston, Texas,** on Wednesday as **Mexican** and **Haitian** troops traded fire in a third day of battles during which more than 50 civilians died.

"Explosions rocked the city center as dozens of rockets traced red-lines across the sky, silhouetted by oil-drilling rigs, and the clatter of small arms fire, the deafening noise of RPGs (rocket-propelled grenades), light and heavy mortars sent Houston residents running for cover or kept them crouching in their homes."

Mexicans and Haitians, former allies who invaded America to get rid of its president and insure their own "security," turned their guns against each other over the control of the American city of Houston.

How would the American people react to the above story? What would the United Nations do?

Would the World Bank still give loans to Mexico and Haiti if they had invaded America, and while they were engaged in fighting over the American "black diamond" (oil) City of Houston?

Even though the above is fictional, as far as Houston, Texas is concerned, this is exactly what is presently taking place in the Democratic Republic of the Congo:

- Rwanda, Uganda, and Burundi have invaded the Congo, and are over 700 miles deep inside the Congo away from their borders and are, as reported by *Reuters* on *June 7th, 2000,* fighting each other over control of the Diamond mining Congolese City of Kisangani.
- On the same day, June 7th, 2000, as reported by *Bloomberg News* of Washington, DC, *"Rwanda Gets World Bank Loans Even as UN Condemns Congo Fighting."*
- As everyone knows, NOBODY gets a dollar from the World Bank without the approval of the United States administration.
- Thus, those killed in the Congo are credited to President Clinton. Why? Because, first, he gives direct American financial and military support to Uganda and Rwanda and allows white American mercenaries to fight alongside their armies. Second, he allows world institutions to continue to give monies to these countries that have violated the INTERNATIONALLY SACRED RULES OF *TERRITORIAL INTEGRITY AND NATIONAL SOVEREIGNITY* in regard to the Congo, a country that has neither provoked Rwanda, Uganda, Burundi, nor participated in the internal and perennial ethnic wars that have been taking place in these three countries.
- Most importantly, everyone knows that if President Clinton orders, today, that Uganda and Rwanda leave the Congo, they will do so. Neither Uganda, nor Rwanda, nor Burundi who are engaged in inter-ethnic wars in their respective countries, would dare go to war against a country over ten times its own size in the case of Uganda, and one hundred times in the case of Rwanda or Burundi.

The United States of America, which engineered an international coalition of nations in order to extirpate Iraq out of Kuwait, and bomb the Serbians out of Kosovo, is supporting militarily, financially, and economically Uganda, Rwanda, and Burundi, who have invaded the Democratic Republic of the Congo.

The killing, raping, burning, torturing of Black women and the cold-blooded killing of Black children, the elderly, and men in the Congo is happening because President Bill Clinton and his Western allies are allowing it.

Item: UNITED NATIONS, June 9, 2000 (*Reuters*)-Anthony Goodman reports: "1.7 million die in eastern Congo due to war."

Question: Why is it that the simplest, the easiest conflict that Clinton and the West could resolve, they let it fester to the point of the death toll reaching into the millions?

Answer: It is because those who are dying are Black, Africans. Pure and simple!

If they were white, the whole Western European and the American governments and media would have been up in arms and would have had daily lead stories of moving images, photographs of the dead, the raped, the burned, the mutilated, and the grieving. There would have followed resolutions, executive decisions, military mobilizations, and ultimatums to the invaders to get out or else.

Alas, the Congolese are Black. What do white governments have to lose? No white lives or soldiers have to die for Blacks, except the mercenaries who are not known to the public.

In fact, the West and America have everything to gain: Congolese diamonds, gold, manganese, cobalt, and rare minerals for cheap. The millions being made from these minerals acquired through the blood of Congolese children, women, and the elderly are being used to finance the elections in America and Europe. Thus the politicians and governments shut up. These millions shut them up. Consequently, for fear of losing these millions, no politician dares speak out, show outrage, and demand action over the killing of Blacks in Africa.

Acknowledgements

I would like to acknowledge and thank those organizations that think it necessary to expose crimes, injustices, and untold suffering that take place in countries that have been marginalized by the major media outlets of the technologically most advanced countries.

The information provided herein comes from many of these organizations. In addition, on a daily basis, the syndicated news gathering agencies report on what is taking place in countries such as the Democratic Republic of the Congo. Reports such as those of the Amnesty International, Reuters syndicated news, Bloomberg syndicated news, The Associated Press, and many religious agencies and news organizations.

This book could not have been possible without the information gathered and published by The Ministry of Human Rights of the Democratic Republic of the Congo.

All the evidences, including photographs of murder, torture, rape, and other atrocities that the Ministry published in the series called "Livre Blanc" have been confirmed by independent news agencies, human rights monitoring organizations like Amnesty International, and many other religious organizations.

We used the Information from the *Livre Blanc*'s *Tomes 2 and 3,* as well as the *Livre Blanc Special (August 1999),* and the *Livre Blanc* covering the period of August 2, 1998 to November 5, 1998. These books were published and distributed as public information under the leadership of Mr. Leonard SHE OKITUNDU, Congolese Minister of Human Rights.

The pictures in this book come exclusively from the "Livre Blanc" series. We thank the Ministry of Human Rights for making them available.

The "Livre Blancs" were written in French. Any part used in this book is the author's translation.

The author wishes to thank all those who helped in gathering this information and making it available to the public. May their benevolent work for the sake of true justice inspire those who read this book and make them spring into action and help end the nightmare being visited on the innocent Congolese people.

1

Introduction

This book is written to appeal to all humans who are against injustice, genocide, exploitation, and pure greed.

In this New Millennium, year 2000, one would think, one would believe, one would hope, one would indeed expect that the only Superpower left on earth, The United States of America, the beacon of democratic ideals, would oppose and go all out against or help prevent genocide everywhere in the world in the same manner it had done in selected places. Unfortunately, this has not been the case.

Those of us, who live in America and know about American politics, would hear the brouhaha of those who would say, "Well, you cannot expect America to police the whole world!" But the Truth, if it can be told, is that the "world policeman" argument is selectively voiced by those who are either racist to the core, or ignorant to the bones.

To tell these two apart one has to search their lives and see what stands they have taken in the past on similar issues. As regard the *racist to the core*, one can tell them by finding out, for instance, whether they supported America's bombing in Kosovo to stop ethnic cleansing; America's war to dislodge Iraq out of Kuwait and its subsequent bombings inside

1

Iraq itself, to cite but these two cases. If they did, then you know where their racism lies.

As for those who may be *ignorant to the bones,* one can easily tell them apart because they oppose any action and every action that the United States takes internationally. For them, the United States should mind the United States' affairs only and should not get involved in other countries' business. This category opposes, for instance, The United States' efforts to bring peace to Ireland or to Palestine between the Israelis and the Arabs; or even for the US to fund famine relief programs in the Third World.

This last category forgets that the USA, though a superpower, depends on less powerful nations for the resources that the daily lives of Americans require. Without these resources, the superpower status of the USA would easily be put to risk. This is why America cannot afford to be isolationistic or autarchic.

Fortunately, in America, foreign policy is a matter of the administration in place. In the United States system of government, no matter what some racist citizens or elected officials may say, foreign policy is the prerogative of the Executive Branch of government. Meaning, the President of the United States decides what kind of foreign policy he (pardon the gender "he" but there has not been a "she" president yet) is going to have, and what military campaigns he is going to involve the American troops and to what extent. The clear demarcation between the three branches of the American system of government is not only the reason why America endures no matter what kind of presidents, congresspeople and senators, or judges pass this way, but it is also the reason why an American president cannot hide behind the US Congress or the Senate for his failure on foreign policy.

As the history of the United States clearly bears it out, every president has left his own particular stamp or unique legacy, as far as American foreign policy is concerned.

The question we are, here, posing is whether *Murder, Rape, and misery* would constitute *President Clinton's Congo Legacy?*

We are going to put forth the facts as they stand today in the Democratic Republic of the Congo. We are going to show the United States' role in the events taking place there, viz., the war in the East of the Congo, which has been called "Africa's World War," whatever this means. Specifically, we are going to bare out the Clinton Administration's responsibility in the atrocities being committed in the Congo and the suffering of the Congolese people.

We understand how things work in America. We know that, in America, the government and the media influence the people's collective mind, collective knowledge, and collective reactions and actions. Hence, what the government and the media does not want the people to know, they keep it away from the people. And when the government and the media want the American people to rise up either against or for some issue, they whip the people into non-stop frenzy with that issue, day in and day out.

The above can be easily demonstrated by the recent case of the young Cuban boy, Elian. The whole world knows that the entire American government and media were mobilized on one side or the other of the Elian's case, whether he should stay with his relatives in Miami, USA, or be returned to his father in Cuba. On the other hand, the US government and the media, deliberately and conspiratorially, kept under wrap, therefore the world knows very little that, in the Congo, fifteen Congolese women were buried alive by the United States backed Rwandan and Ugandan armed forces, because these women had the dignity to refuse to be raped by these men who were not their husbands.

Even though the State Department, the CIA, therefore the Washington Post, the New York Times, CBS, NBC, ABC, and all the major media outlets were privy to this information, they did not want it out, thus, they kept it away from the American people. Thus, it is as if what happened to these Congolese women never took place, while we, in America, were driven into the drunkenness of Elian Gonzales's world-shattering fate.

We hope that what follows will inform those who do not know that something terrible is happening on this earth, in this day and age, something that the American government and the media are not telling us. That the US government is keeping from its citizens the atrocities being committed by countries that receive money from the American taxpayer. Hopefully, either the government or the media will come out forcefully and do something about it, if not for the sake of basic justice, at least for the sake of humanity, for the sake of basic human dignity, when the evidence is laid before the world.

Moreover, America needs to learn from Europe, which is learning the hard way, with the backfiring of its racist policies intended to destabilize and continually impoverish black Africa, and install, in Black African countries, puppets who let Europe have its way with African resources.

Europe's African policies have led to the increased misery that has driven the Africans to the very European countries that are responsible for this misery in the first place. Now Europeans are up in arms that too many Africans are migrating to Europe.

As President Bill Clinton's second and last term draws to a close, what is going to be his Congo legacy? As far as the Congolese people are concerned, if his presidency ended today, his legacy would be negative and destructive to the Congolese people, and the name Clinton would for ever be associated with murder, torture, rape, hunger, and misery by proxy through Uganda, Rwanda and Burundi.

Fortunately, there are, still, a few months to go before Bill Clinton leaves the office of the president of the United States. And, as it will be shown in the following pages, President Clinton can end his term with the Congolese people being left alone, at peace, independent and sovereign to decide on their future for themselves and by themselves.

Simply and categorically stated, President Clinton has the power to stop the atrocities in the Congo any day. Today. Right now, if he so will.

2

Reading President Bill Clinton on the Congo

We have not talked with President Clinton. If we had done so before putting together the evidences gathered here, we would have asked him some questions. His answers would have allowed us to determine his motivation, his reasons for letting, tolerating, and supporting Rwanda, Uganda and Burundi in their invasion and occupation of part of the Congo, and in their carrying this genocide against the Congolese people, with the Congo's minerals and other resources being stolen from the occupied areas by both these three countries and the American and European corporations operating there.

Some of the questions we would have asked President Clinton would have been of the nature for us to find out:

Whether Mr. Clinton is a racist or does not care for Africans, even though it appears that he could not be a racist since Congolese, like Ugandans, Rwandans and Burundians, are all Black people. In fact, Mr. Clinton's record in America tells us that many of his friends, associates, and cabinet members are black. Unless…

Whether Mr. Clinton is sympathetic to and supports the Rwanda-Burundi-Ugandan invasion and occupation of the Congo and does not condemn or stop them from murdering and committing these atrocities on the Congolese people, because he blames the Congo for the 1994 genocide of the *Rwandan* Hutus on their countrymen, the *Rwandan* Tutsis. We would think that he would not do so, since, as president of the USA, he has the best information possible and **he knows** (or should know) that this genocide was carried out by *Rwandan* people, the Hutus, on other *Rwandan* people, the Tutsis, inside *Rwandan* territory. No Congolese was involved in it, directly or indirectly. We would hope that President Clinton is informed that Rwandan Hutus and Tutsis have been killing one another, back and forth, for a long time since their colonial masters, the Belgians, set one group against the other. We would dare trust that Mr. Clinton knows that in 1994, the Hutus started killing the Tutsis (and France, the US, and the UN could have prevented it) because the ones suspected their brethren Tutsis of assassinating Juvenal Habyarimana, the then-Rwandan president who was of Hutu lingual group. And now, the United Nations investigations have shown that Paul Kagame, a Tutsi and the now-president of Rwanda and the top military leader when Abyarimana was assassinated, may have ordered the shooting down of the airplane carrying Mr. Abyarimana. This means that no Congolese have ever been involved in this back-and-forth co-genocide between Hutus and Tutsis in Rwanda, Uganda, and Burundi.

Whether Mr. Clinton is so pro-multinationals and so pro-white conglomerates that he does not care how many Congolese women are raped, burned or buried alive, how many Congolese children and elderly are killed, and how many Congolese men are killed, mutilated, or tortured. The only thing mattering for President Clinton, not that these wealthy giants negotiate and pay a fair price for Congo's minerals, but that they acquire these minerals and other resources, at the cheapest price that they want to spend, meaning, the blood, death, and misery of the Congolese people, not with US dollars. Some of these conglomerates being BOSUCO, LITTLEROCK MINING LIMITED, TENFIELD HOLDINGS LIMITED, COLLIER VENTURES LIMITED, SAPORA MINING LIMITED, INTERMARKET LIMITED, BARRICK GOLD CORPORATION, BANRO RUSSEL RESSOURCES MAHILA, LAMBO 1 and KAMPEMBA, JARDIN LAMBO 2 LUFUNGA, and others involved in the diamond, manganese, silver, rare minerals, and other traditional mining interests in the Congo.

Whether President Clinton hates Laurent Kabila, the president of the Congo, or whether President Clinton believes that the US policy toward black African countries is that nobody can lead a black African country unless he is either on the CIA payroll or on that of American's Europeans' allies; and, because Kabila is not in American or European pockets, he must be removed from power, and this is why the American government is, not only supplying Uganda-Rwanda-Burundi with sophisticated weaponry, but is also allowing white mercenaries to fight alongside Rwanda-Uganda-Burundian forces in the Congo where they rape, maim, rob, and kill with impunity.

Whether President Clinton, a well-informed man of high intellect, knows that the United States government is responsible for the Congo being in the bad shape it is in now. How come? Because, as every properly-informed person knows, in 1960, after the Congo snatched its independence from Belgium and democratically elected Patrice Lumumba to lead its government, the American government and its CIA led its allies in killing Lumumba and destabilizing the country, until a "suitable" replacement was found in Mobutu Sese Seko. The latter would be kept in power, by America and its allies, for over 32 years, and America looked the other way while Mobutu killed his own people, starved some of them to death, and, in tandem with international conglomerates, participated in the raping of the Congo's mineral and non-mineral resources, while leaving the Congo and its people in poverty, misery, and degradation. Now, in 1997, Kabila removed Mobutu, and, because Kabila wants independence and sovereignty for his country and his people, he must be killed or be removed. After overthrowing Mobutu, who left the Congo in ruins and without any structure of an organized society, and the people in starvation and without the basic medical necessities, Kabila was never offered any help to either rebuild the country or feed the hungry. No governmental action was taken, in America or in Europe, to help the Congo, recognizing that the plight of the Congolese people was due to American and European policies and support for their stooge, the dictator Mobutu.

As Papa Pugu-Bola, an elderly 80 year-old Congolese and retired teacher asked, in desperation, in Kinshasa, "What is it with 'mindele' that they cannot stand an African 'ndombe' be a free man like any other man, speak out on the sufferings his people have suffered at the hands of the 'mindele' and their agents in Africa, or want to deal with them as equal human beings should do?" "Because," he continued, answering his own question, "you know they decided to kill Lumumba because he gave that little speech in front of Roi Baudouin on the sufferings of his people at the hands of the Belgians, the meaning of true independence, and how the Congolese people were going to build their country and make it more beautiful than before." "And now," he somberly concluded, "they want to kill Kabila, also, because he does not want to be another Mobutu to both his people and to the 'mindele'. But why are these 'mindele' like this?" I tried to tell him that not all the 'mindele' are bad. To which he shot back, "Well, where then are the good ones while we are suffering and dying here?"

Finally, whether President Clinton considers Black Africans inferior and the lives of African women, children, men, and the elderly, not as valuable as the lives of whites. Because, Mr. Clinton seems to follow the advice of his rich friends who have given millions to his political life and who are, at the same time, those with hundreds of millions invested in the companies that are supporting the war in the Congo because they do not believe in negotiating with the Congo government and paying a fair price for the Congo's minerals and other raw materials. It seems like, for these white conglomerates, if an African president does not like the cheap price they want to pay for Africa's wealth, if this African country wants to negotiate for a fairer and better deal, then the conglomerates simply undertake the killing or removing of the African President who dares think himself and his people as equal to the whites. Whether this is also President Clinton's belief.

3

Amnesty International and the Such

On Wednesday, May 31st, 2000, Amnesty International released a report on the atrocities being perpetrated on the Congolese children, women, the elderly, and men.

Titled *"Killing Human Decency,"* Amnesty International documents detailed accounts of the crimes being committed in the Congo against the Congolese people. Instances of torture, rape, murder, execution, and other atrocities.

Many other organizations and agencies have been documenting these crimes. But, we ask, what is it going to take for the international community, for the superpower America, for the other powers, to rise up and put a stop to the sufferings of the Congolese people?

One thing that Amnesty International may or may not say is the following:

In this dying of the Congolese people, Rwanda, Uganda, and Burundi are the aggressors. They invaded the Congo and they should not be in Congo territory. No matter what the excuse, it is untenable. It is inexcusable.

Uganda-Rwanda-Burundi could not have dared invade the Congo and now occupy territories bigger than their own countries without the blessings and military support of the United States of America and the Europeans who are financing these atrocities against the Congolese people.

Almost every week, many other agencies and organizations are reporting the crimes against the Congolese. However, until America and Europe decides that these crimes must stop, no matter how many gruesome reports come out, the killers will continue to kill while Europe and America get their minerals and other resources.

It is no secret that without American and European support, Rwanda, Uganda, and Burundi would not have dared carried out their murderous campaign in the Congo. These three countries together are about ten times smaller than the Congo. Every one of them is bogged down into internal ethnic or, better yet, lingual wars that have been going on for years.

The governments of Europe and America that support Uganda, Rwanda, and Burundi must be called to task for supporting these three renegade states that have been committing the murderous acts being made public daily (but not being reported by the major media in Europe and America).

For instance, in May, the European governments that give financial support to Uganda (The Paris Club) withheld the money for a while because Ugandan and Rwandan troops were fighting each other over the control of the Congolese mining town of Kisangani. In other words, these so-called democratic governments of Europe were telling Uganda, "all right, it's OK that you, Ugandans, Rwandans, and Burundians, have invaded the sovereignty of another country; it's OK that you have occu-pied part of another country's territory; and it's OK that you and us are stealing the gold, diamonds, and other resources from this country whose territorial integrity you have violated. As long as this is what is happening, we are going to keep funding you. But, you cannot turn around and fight each other over this stolen property, which might jeopardize our mutual thievery interests."

Under these hypocritical circumstances on the part of European and American governments, how can the people of the world trust in such words or concepts as "Freedom," "Democracy," "Territorial Integrity," "Non-Interference," and "Non-Aggression"?

4

Genocide

On a daily basis, Congolese people are dying, men, women, and children. This, however, is not making front page news in America, maybe because the US government is the one financing the war against the Congolese by militarily and economically supporting Uganda and Rwanda (and Burundi to a lesser extent). In addition, the main stream media are owned by or interconnected with the conglomerates that are exploiting the Congo's minerals.

In the following pages we are going to cite some of the crimes that have been committed against the Congolese. We are reporting here only those cases that credible and international organizations and non-governmental agencies have documented and reported. This means that many, many more crimes have not been reported.

These cases are documented so that those humans who read about them will act in order to help put an end to these crimes against miserable, destitute, and innocent human beings. This *"Crime against humanity,"* as George Washington Williams called it when ten million Congolese were slaughtered under King Leopold II, must be denounced by all peace, justice, and equality loving people, governments and organizations.

The Congolese are innocent because they have never invaded or sought to occupy the territory of any of its nine bordered neighbors: Congo-Brazzaville, Central African Republic, the Sudan, Uganda, Rwanda, Burundi, Tanzania, Zambia, and Angola. Neither one of these neighbors has either the size or the quantity of the resources that the Congo has.

We strongly believe, as the white Englishman, E.D. MOREL wrote in 1909, in the "Foreword" to his book, *Great Britain and the Congo*, as he almost single-handedly led the worldwide campaign to denounce and expose the genocide of over ten million Congolese by King Leopold II, his associates, shareholders, and agents,

"that in every land men (**and** *women,* **we dare add**)*are to be found, prepared, when they know the facts, to throw themselves in the scale against organized iniquity, the forces of corruption, and the criminal apathy of Governments, and to do the work which those in executive authority have left undone."*

BEHEADED AND CUT OPEN BY THE RWANDAN SOL- DIERS FOR TRYING TO DEFEND A PREGNANT WOMAN FROM BEING KILLED AND CUT OPEN

This photo is of the bodyguard of Mwami (King) MUBEZA III of the town of Kasika. He was murdered in this manner by the Rwandan sol- diers, because he tried to prevent the Rwandans from cutting open the pregnant wife of King or Mwami MUBEZA (so that she will not bare a child who may lay claim to the land of his parents, since Rwandan had plans to annex this part of the Congolese territory).

Is this a lesser atrocity than the ones committed in Kosovo or in Serbia? Is a black life worth less than a white life? Why then are American and European governments still financing Uganda-Burundi-Rwandan invasion and occupation of the Congo by financially and militarily aiding these three countries?

22 YEAR-OLD GIRL KILLED WITH BLOWS TO THE HEAD BY UGANDO-RWANDAN SOLDIERS, AFTER THEY REPEATEDLY RAPED HER UNTIL SHE LOST CONSCIOUSNESS

Ugandan and Rwandan troops that took over the town of Kavumu, in the region of Bukavu, kidnapped the 22 year-old Miss. Nicole MIKUNGA. They repeatedly raped her, helping themselves one after another until the young woman lost consciousness. Then, to shut her mouth for good so that she never testify against them, she was killed with blows to her head.

Is this a lesser atrocity than the ones committed in Kosovo or in Serbia? Is a black life worth less than a white life? Why then are American and European governments still financing Uganda-Burundi-Rwandan invasion and occupation of the Congo by financially and militarily aiding these three countries?

A 74-YEAR-OLD ELDERLY MAN SHOT AND LEFT TO ROT IN THE OPEN AS AN EXAMPLE TO OTHERS.
HIS CRIME: AS THE CLAN ELDER, HE REFUSED TO ALLOW HIS GRANDCHILDREN TO FORCEFULLY JOIN THE RWANDAN-UGANDAN ARMY AND FIGHT OTHER CONGOLESE

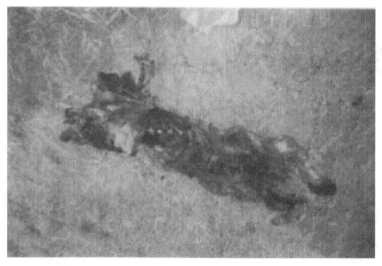

This photo shows the decomposing body of "Vieux" (old man) TEN-GENESHA BIBIHERI, 74 years old. He was assassinated point blank by Rwandan soldiers in the town of Kalemie, north of Katanga. As the elder of the family, he refused to give permission for his grandchildren to join the Rwandan-Ugandan forces, then turn around and go fight other Congolese. So, as an example to those in town and a reminder that they must do what they are told, "old-man" TENGENESHA was shot dead, and his body ordered not to be buried, in order for everyone in the town to either see or smell his decomposing body.

Is this a lesser atrocity than the ones committed in Kosovo or in Serbia? Is a black life worth less than a white life? Why then are American and European governments still financing Uganda-Burundi-Rwandan invasion and occupation of the Congo by financially and militarily aiding these three countries?

AFTER HAVING RAPED WOMEN, THEIR HEADS AND BREASTS WERE CUT OFF AND THEY WERE THROWN IN THE RIVER

The soldiers from Uganda, Rwanda, and Burundi found no resistance in Congolese towns, as far as military confrontation was concerned. But the Congolese, even though unarmed, refused to be violated and raped by these soldiers, because, like all other humans, they do have the dignity to preserve their bodies for their chosen partners. Because they refused to be raped, pregnant women were forcibly raped, then their heads and breasts were cut off before being thrown in rivers. (This reminds one of the pictures that were seen on television, in 1994, what Rwandans were doing to other Rwandans, in Rwanda).

Is this a lesser atrocity than the ones committed in Kosovo or in Serbia? Is a black life worth less than a white life? Why then are American and European governments still financing Uganda-Burundi-Rwandan invasion and occupation of the Congo by financially and militarily aiding these three countries?

MEN, WHEN KILLED, WERE PUT TOGETHER AND SET AFIRE SO AS NOT TO BE IDENTIFIED BY THEIR RELATIVES, A PRACTICE CALLED *"QUARTIER"*

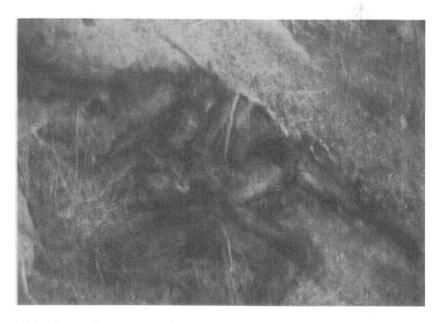

This photo shows men who were rounded up by Ugandan-Rwandan forces, in the town of Kalemie, in the north of Katanga. After they were shot dead, they were put together and then torched up, so they could burn and not be recognized by either their family members, or anyone else who might try to identify them by names.

Is this a lesser atrocity than the ones committed in Kosovo or in
Serbia? Is a black life worth less than a white life? Why then are
American and European governments still financing Uganda-Burundi-
Rwandan invasion and occupation of the Congo by financially and mil-
itarily aiding these three countries?

The Rwandan-Ugandan-Burundian soldiers, when they do not like a
household because of the attitude of the parents or their refusal to
cooperate with the invaders, will kill the entire family and then set them
afire. In this photo, members of a family were burned together; including two children aged five and six.

Is this a lesser atrocity than the ones committed in Kosovo or in
Serbia? Is a black life worth less than a white life? Why then are American
and European governments still financing Uganda-Burundi-Rwandan
invasion and occupation of the Congo by financially and militarily aiding these three countries?

KILLED FOR PROTECTING THE NATIONAL PARC OF VIRUNGA AND ITS RARE SPECIES OF ENDANGERED LIFE FORMS

The National Park of Virunga is home to many endangered species of the African fauna. And, for trying to reason with the Rwandan-Ugandan invaders on the importance of protecting and preserving these rare species, Mr. MUHINGO MATIMANO was shot dead, and his body left there on the ground in front of the entrance to the park.

Is this a lesser atrocity than the ones committed in Kosovo or in Serbia? Is a black life worth less than a white life? Why then are American and European governments still financing Uganda-Burundi-Rwandan invasion and occupation of the Congo by financially and militarily aiding these three countries?

AMERICAN INSTITUTIONS OF HIGHER LEARNING AND NASA IN CONPLICITY WITH THE RWANDANS INVADERS OF CONGO TERRITORY:

WHILE THE LEGITIMATE CONGOLESE OWNERS AND GUARDIANS OF THESE AREAS ARE BUTCHERED (as in the picture above), AMERICANS STAY MUM AND, SHAMELESSLY AND UNETHICALLY, JOIN THE RWANDANS IN EXPLOITING CONGO'S FAUNA SUCH AS THE MOUNTAIN GORILLAS IN THE VIRUNGA CONSERVATION AREA THAT MOSTLY LAY WAY INSIDE CONGOLESE TERRITORY NOW OCCUPIED BY RWANDA AND IS OUT OF MINUSCULE RWANDA ITSELF.

The most blatant example of this can be seen and read in The New York Times' article of Tuesday, April 11, 2000 edition, page F3, titled "Tracking Gorillas and Rebuilding a Country," by James Glanz.

These Americans with Rwandans, are tracking gorillas in three countries, yet talking about rebuilding the country with the tiniest part of the conservation area.

"In August (of 1999?), researchers found just how strikingly detailed the vegetation maps could be when they flew over about 100 square miles in the Virungas, **including parts of all three of the countries that contain it,…**"

In August 1998, Rwanda had invaded and occupied the part of the Congo that includes the Virungas. Are these Americans lending legitimacy to Rwandan occupation of the Congo? What a shame, joining in a criminal, unethical, and an act surely unbecoming of institutions of higher learning and of international scope like NASA.

Do these Americans expect Rwanda to annex the Congolese territory forever or what?

The article talks of a collaboration "of severak American and Rwandan institutions" only. No Congolese persons or institutions are mentioned as participators in the project.

The institutions participating include, according to The New York Times article are, the Dian Fossey Gorilla Fund International, the National University of Rwanda, the Georgia Institute of Technology, Clark Atlanta University, Zoo Atlanta and a number of Rwandan government agencies."

Much of the money for the project comes from the Georgia Research Alliance ($300,000). NASA's Digital Earth Initiative "is also supporting the project."

Maybe purposefully, none of the three whites (2 males and one female) and two Black males on the photo accompanying the article are identified by name. Only the gorilla's name, Ruhuka, is mentioned.

What a shame to these higher institutions, in the Land of Democracy and of higher academic ethics!

KIDNAPPED, TAKEN TO UGANDA, TORTURED AND DIED FROM HIS INJURIES FOR SIGNING A COLLECTIVE LETTER PROTESTING RWANDAN ANNEXATION OF THE CONGOLESE PROVINCE OF NORTH KIVU

MR. DESIRE LUMBU LUMBU

Mr. DESIRE LUMBU LUMBU was an honorary minister of Social Services in the government of the second Congolese Republic (when the country was called Zaire). He was arrested from his own house on

Sunday, November 14, 1999, around 1:00 PM. He was taken to the headquarters of the Ugandan intelligence division in the Congo. Around 3:00 PM of the same day, he was taken to Kampala, the capital of Uganda, along with another prisoner: MR KASEREKA KIHUVI.

In Kampala, both men were subjected to long interrogations, torture, inhumanely mistreated and degraded. The injuries he suffered at the hands of his torturers led to his death in the town of Beni.

The reason for his imprisonment, torture and ultimate death was that his community initiated a collective letter protesting Rwanda's annexation of the Congolese Province of North Kivu.

Mr. Armand THAMBA VANGU

Mr. VANGU, a officer with the Catholic organization CARITAS in the Town of Uvira.

He was assassinated in the front of the French Cultural Center.

How many more have to be killed before the world, the so-called democracies, react?

15 WOMEN BURIED ALIVE (For refusing to become sex slaves and to be raped)

Between the 15th and thee 22nd of November, 1999, as the Rwandan-Burundian-Ugandan forces roamed through the territory of Mwenga, in the province of South Kivu, in the subdivisions of Bulinzi, of Bogombe, and of Ngando, their viciousness was demonstrated in the manner in which these soldiers punished the women who resisted being raped.

A sample of what these invaders have been doing is illustrated in the case of the following fifteen women, in different villages in this region, who were subjected to the same type of torture and death. When they resisted these soldiers, they were, first, beaten, then African hot pepper was rubbed all over their bodies' wounds and inserted through every orifice of their bodies: eyes, mouths, noses, ears, anus, and vaginas, in order to make these women suffer. Then, the women were buried alive.

Following are their names and hometowns:

1. Evelyne BITONDO, from the town of BULINDJI;
2. MBILINZI MUSOMBWA, from the town of BULINZI;
3. Christine SAFI, from the town of Bulinzi;
4. Aniece KUNGWA, from the town of Bulinzi;
5. Monique NAKUSU NAKIPIMO, from the town of Bulinzi;
6. TABU WAKENGE, from the town of Ilinda;
7. NYASSA KASANDULE, from the town of Ilinda;
8. MAPENDO MUTITU, from the town of Ilinda;
9. BUKUMBU, from the town of Ilinda;
10. Spouse MWAMI KISALI;
11. Maman SIFA;
12. Maman MUKOTO;
13. The still unidentified body of a woman;
14. MUKUNDA, from the town of Bongombe;
15. MBILINZI KIANDUNDU, from the town of Ngando.

MASSACRE IN MAKOBOLA:
818 CIVILIAN MEN, WOMEN, THE ELDERLY, AND CHILDREN BUTCHERED BY THE COMBINED FORCES OF RWANDA, UGANDA, AND BURUNDI IN THE CONGO

It took Amnesty International more than a year to publish its report that detailed some of the atrocities that the occupying forces of Rwanda, Uganda, and Burundi have been committing in the Congo. These three countries now effectively occupy most of the northeast and southeast of the Congo, and they are involved in the policy of killing , depopulating the areas bordering their countries so that they can, by default, annex them.

Are America and Europe waiting for Congolese children, women, the elderly, and men to die in the hundreds of thousands before they order their blood-thirsty clients (Uganda-Rwanda-Burundi) to get out of the Congo, so that the massacres, rapes, mutilations, and tortures can stop?

One of the cases that Amnesty International reports took place in January 1999. It is the *MASSACRE IN MAKOBOLA*, in the territory of FIZI, in the province of South Kivu now almost entirely occupied by the combined forces of Rwanda, Burundi and Uganda.

Below is a table that documents this crime, giving the individual names of the victims, their age, and the name of their hometowns.

TABLE OF NAMES				
NBR	NAMES OF MASSACRED PEOPLE	Age	SEX	Village
01	ABUNGU CHRISTINE	-	F	MIKUNGA
02	AMANI LUSUNGU	-	m	"
03	AWEZAYE KAHINDO	-	F	"
04	AMISA NAMLANGALO	-	F	"
05	APOLINA BYOSAA	-	F	"
06	ASENDE MASUMBUKO	-	F	"
07	ALUMBE MUKOKO	-	F	BANGWE
08	ABWE MULASHI	-	F	"
09	ALIMASI LUMENGE	-	m	"
10	ASANI ALUMBE	-	m	"
11	ALINGI ONGEMBALAMWEGI	-	m	"
12	APAKO	-	F	"
13	ATONDA	-	F	"
14	AAMBA SALUMUMBALAMWECHI	-	m	"
15	AMISI ABUNGO	-	F	"
16	ABWE ISHIABWE	-	-M	"
17	ANGELAN MALIPO	-		"
18	ALISA NYAMGO	-	F	KAHAMA
19	ANTO LOTOELO	-	F	"
20	ABELECI LOTOELO	-	m	"
21	AMISA LOTOELO	-	F	"
22	ASENDE SELEMANI	-	F	"
23	ABWE YALUMBA	-	m	"
24	ARONILUTUMBU	-	m	"
25	ABALE ILANGYI	-	m	NGALULA
26	AOCI MMANINWA	-	m	"
27	AMBAMBA MMANINWA	-	m	MBOKO
28	ABEBELE MAWAZO	-	F	KASHEKEZI
29	AMUNASO MULISHO	-	F	KASHEKEZI
30	ASSUMANI HALI	-	m	"
31	ABABELE ALISHI	-	m	"
32	ALISA WABANGWA	-	F	KIVONGOLWA
33	ABWE FAHISI	-	m	"
34	ALUMBE ABINAMWISHO	-	F	KAMBA
35	ALUNGU LOKOLE	-	m	"
36	ASSANIALEXI	-	M	KASHEKEZI
37	ALUNGU ONGE		m	"
38	ADOLPHE OMARI	5y.o.	M	KALOMO
39	AMBA SALUMU		m	"
40	ABALE ONGEMBALA	46y.o.	F	BANGWE
41	A GELA LSALUMU	45y.o.	F	"

42	ALULEYA ABALE GANA	20y.o.	M	BANGWE
43	ALUBETINA ABABELE		F	"
44	ALUMBE KA		M	"
45	ALUTA YENA		F	"
46	ASENDE ESOA	7 y.o.	F	MIKUNGA
47	ABUNGO WILONGA	42y.o.		"
48	AMISA ELOCO	5 y.o.	F	"
49	AOCINENDJO	4 y.o.	M	MIKUNGA
50	AKUMBA OREDI	6 y.o.	M	"
51	ASENDE ELISA	10y.o.	F	"
52	ALONDA MWAMI CHANGA	30y.o.	M	"
53	ABEKYA IYANGYA	67y.o.	M	"
54	ABULE LUSAKANYA	18y.o.	M	"
55	AKUMA ABEKYA	1y.o.	M	"
56	APENDEKI MIRENGE KASONGO	40y.o.	F	KATUTA
57	APENDEKIGERARD	12y.o.	M	"
58	APENDE KI LUMINA	31 y.o.	F	"
59	AOCI LUMINA	8y.o.	M	"
60	ABABELE MBELECI	18y.o.	F	K.ASHEKEZI
61	AMAZO ECINA	40y.o.	F	"
62	ASSUMANI ECA	6y.o.	M	"
63	AMBAMBE PILIMO		M	MUKWEZI
64	AMSINI PIPA	40y.o.	M	MUNENE
65	APOLINA MITAMBA	38y.o.	F	"
66	ASUKULU SANTO	1y.o.	M	"
67	ANDRESLOBONGYA	55y.o.	M	KAHAMA
68	ANDALA TITO	8y.o.	M	"
69	ALONDA POPO	1Oy.o.	M	"
70	ASUKULU POPO	6y.o.	M	"
71	ALISA WAESUBE	7y.o.	F	NGALULA
72	ALISA BITENDELO	43y.o.	F	"
73	ABUBAKAR MUSTAFA	-	M	KAMBA
74	ALLY MOUSTAPHAN	-	M	"
75	ASENDE MUNDA	-	M	"
76	AMISSI JUMA	-	M	"
77	ABWE ANGELE	-	M	"
78	ALULEYA AKYAKALA	-	M	"
79	AMOSSI MAHASHA	-	M	"
80	ASUKULU PAUL	-	M	"
81	BUDOGOBUDOGO (Burundian refugee)	-	F	MAKOBOLA
82	BAHATI BULENGE	-	M	"
83	BYAOMBE CESAR	-	M	"
84	BILOMBELE EBENGO	-	F	KATUTA
85	BITA KAHINDO	-	M	MIKUNGA
86	BIENFAIT ITONGWA		M	"
87	BILEMO SALEHE		F	"
88	BILEBWA MAWAZO		M	"
				"

89	BUHEBELU LANKINA		F	MIKUNGA
90	BOSONGOMA MAYALIWA		m	"
91	BINWA BITA		m	"
92	BOBILYA ABWE MBALAMWESHI		F	"
93	BOKOBO LWAMESSO		m	"
94	BOBILYA BAKUMBA		F	"
95	BILOMBELE LOTOELO		F	kAHAMA
96	BONYEMU LOTOELO		F	"
97	BYALUNWA ABWE	-	F	"
98	BYALUNWA ICIBYANGYLA	-	m	"
99	BULUMBA ISHEKELA	-	F	"
100	BULEMBO SADI	-	F	"
101	BUSA MBILIZI	-	m	"
102	BILOMBELE NYASSA	-	F	NGALULA
103	BAHATI		M	MUKWEZI
104	BITISHO MAWAZO	-	F	KASENYA
105	BIBI NAKITUNGA	-	F	"
106	BELLE FILLE MIKOMA	-	F	KALOMO
107	BAIYE JOSEPHINE	-	F	ILAKALA
106	BENJAMIN SHIABWE	-	m	"
109	BENGA JEAN PIERRE	1.8y.o.	M	BANGWE
110	BAUKYAKA ECUMBE	30y.o.	F	"
111	BUYEMBU WIYONGA	32y.o.	m	"
112	BUNYEMU ELOKO	8y.o.	M	MIKUNGA
113	BILEMO ITONGWA	9y.o.	F	"
114	BATASEMA BWALFU	14y.o.	m	"
115	BILECA APENDEKI	5y.o.	F	"
116	BULOKO MWA A	3y.o.	m	"
117	BYAOMBE BAELANYA	3y.o.	F	"
118	BAHINGWASE YOHERI	5y.o.	M	KATUTA
119	BORA BARUTI,	15y.o.	F	"
120	BWENGE LUMINA	4y.o.	m	"
121	BALULU LUMINA	1y.o.	m	"
122	BAHATI MASUMBUKO		M	MUKWEZI
123	BAHIYE YONA	49y.o.	F	MUNENE
124	BIBYANE ITONGWA	3y.o.	F	KAHAMA
125	BOLENGELWA ALENGE	4y.o.	m	"
126	BENOIS	46y.o.	m	"
127	BOKABO RAMAZANI	37y.o.	M	NGALULA
128	BYAUSSA BYASONGA	77y.o.	m	"
129	BILOMBELE ANGELANI	-	F	KAMBA
130	BAHELANYA MANYANGA	-	m	"
131	BYA M NONI ROSA	-	F	"
132	BULIMWENGU MASHAKA	-	m	"
133	BUKURU SOBANUKA	-	m	"
134	C UDINE BELINDA BENGA	-	F	BANGWE
135	CHEKANABO LOTOELO	-	F	KAHAMA

136	CHEKANABO WILONGA.		F	KAHAMA
137	CHRISTINA		IF	MUNIENE
138	CHALA BILEMU		F	KAMBA
139	CHALA MUSHO		F	KASHEKEZI
140	CHALA ELOGO	37y.o.	F	BANGWO
141	CHALA ELOCO	35y.o.	F	MIKUNGA
141	CHENGA MWANDAMA	9mths	M	KASHEKEZI
142	DEPE LOTOELO		M	KAHAMA
143	DIEUDONNE WALUENYA		M	"
144	DUNIA GODET		m	"
145	DODOMA KATONDA	4y.o.	M	MIKUNGA
146	DESHATI MIRENGE KASONGO	9y.o.	M	KATUTA
147	DIEUDONNE WATEKWA	13y.o.	M	NGALULA
148	DUNIA JEROME		M	KAMBA
149	EPOUSE DIE M. NGWETO		F	MAKOBOLAI
150	EPOUSE DIE M. MANDEVU		F	"
151	ECHA MWENDA		IF	"
152	EYANGANO BIKOPO		F	KATUTA
153	ESOA REMIE		M	MIKUNGA
154	ESOA ONGA OBE		F	"
155	ETO ASONGO		IF	BANGWE
156	ESUBE GASTON		M	KAHAMA
157	ELOCHO LOTOELO		F	"
158	EKYOCHI WABUCIBWA			"
159	EKYOCHINASENDE		IF	"
160	EMBETE LUTUMBA		m	"
161	EKUKULA NDALO		m	"
162	ENDANI TSHEKELA		F-	NGALULA
163	EKA KAMULEWA		M	"
164	EKIKI TUBANGYO		M	KASHEKEZI
165	ESOLOMWA BALAHIMU		m	"
166	ELECHI MASUMBUKO		M	KIVONGOLWA
167	EPANGYA		M	KAMBA
168	ELEMA YAMSHINGA		M	"
169-	EANGANO		F	"
170	ENGENISHI BWANGA	2y.o.	F	ILAKALA
171'	ECHA MWASHITE	3y.o.	IF	BANGWE
172	EPANGYA SALEHE		M	"
173	EPONDO MWA A'	7y.o.	F	MIKUNGA
174	EBISHWA BALONGELWA	9y.o.	m	"
175	ECHULE ITONGWA	1y.o.	m	"
176	ESPERANCE MIRENGE KASONGO	16y.o.	IF	KATUTA
177	EKYOSHI SHINGONDE	14y.o.	M	KASHEKEZI
178	ELISHA ANDO'OLO	31y.o.	m	"
179	ECHA MMBEMBE	3y.o.	F.	"
180,	ESOMBOLA BULAHIMU	63y.o.	m	"
181	ETUNGANO	-	M	MUKWEZI
182	ESPERANCE JOHALI	6y.o.	F	KAHAMA

183	ELISHABETH ITONGWA	1y.o.	F	KAHAMA
184	ESUBE GASTON	55y.o.	M	NGALULA
185	EYANGANO STEFANO		M	KAMBA
186	ELIE JEROME		M	"
187	FITINA FATUMA		F	MAKOBOLAI
188	FATUMA MARONDO		F	KATUTA
189	FITINA NABASIKYAKA		F	MIKUNGA
190	FAMBA LUKOLE		m	"
191	FARAJA ISHEKELA		M	**KAHAMA**
192	FEZA LUTUMBU		F	"
193	**FALIALA MMANDAMA**		m	"
194	FIKIRINI MUFULERO		M	KABUMBE
195	FILIPO ISA		M	NGALULA
196	FAMILY KIHEKA (5children)			
197	FAMILY MANDEVU (2 children)			
198	FITINA FATUMA (2 children)			
199	FAMILY MBIRIMA EMMANUEL (3 chldrn)			
200	FAMILY HOJA BWENGA (4 children)			
201	FAMILY HOJA BWENGA (4 children)			
202	FAMILY MALIYANI GODEFROID (6 chldrn)			
203	FAMILY MIKOMA (9 PERSONS)			
204	FAMILY SEGERE (4 PERSONS)			
205	FAMILY KANGERE (4 PERSONS)			
206	FAMILY WENYA (3 PERSONS)			
207	FAMILY BASHAHUNGU (28 PERSONS)			
208	FAMILY BASHIHOGE (20 PERSONS)			
209	SON OF JOSEPHINE NAOHI (2 PERSONS)			
210	SON OF CHALA (5 PERSONS)			
211	FREDERIC ANGETE	30y.o.	M	MIKUNGA
212	FITINA NAIYANGA	9y.o.	F	"
213	FITINA NASHAGALI	3y.o.	F	KATUTA
.214	FURAHA SANGO	9y.o.	M	KASHEKEZI
215	FURAHA NALUBELA	**4mths**	F	NGALULA
216	FAR IALA APATA	70y.o.	m	"
217	FATUMA MOUSTAN		F	KAMBA
218	GEORGETTE MBYULA		F	MIKUNGA
219	GODETSENGE		F	
220	GANA GANA		M	BANGWE
221	HONORE NAKITUMBA		M	MAKOBOLAI
222	HENRINGOLO		M	BANGWE
223	HERIASUKULU		M	NGALULA
224	HUZURI AMISI	2y.o.	M	MIKUNGA
225	HONORINA MANENO	**3.3y.o.**	F	MIKUNGA
226	HERI MUSASECHA	17y.o.	M	KAHAMA
227	HASHA ANDRE	69y.o.	F	
228	ILEMBO SADI		m	

229	ITONGWA LUNGELE		m	
230	ISMAELBENGA		M	NGALULA
231	IBUCHWA ASUSU		m	"
232	ISHIBABU -		m	"
233	ISHIABWE ASA		M	KASHEKEZI'
234	IDI MIRENGE		m	"
235	ITONGWA NKABO	69y.o.	M	MIKUNGA
236	ISSA LUBUNGA	56y.o.	m	MIKUNGA
237	ISAKA MISABEO	73y.o.	M	KASHEKEZI
238	IOIBUMBA STEPHANE		M	KAMBA
239	JOSEPHINE (Mr. MASTA's wife)		F	MAKOBOLAI
240	JEAN PIERRE KAHINDO		M	MIKUNGA
241	JEANINE MPENDA		F	"
242	JOSEPHINE NA'MMBUTU		F	"
243	JACQUES MWENDA		M	BANGWE
244	JEANNE NDAHAZA		F	KAHAMA
245	JEANNETTE AMBIANCE		F	NGALULA
246	JOSEPH MPUPU		M	MUKWEZI
247	JULIENNE NANGYICHI		F	KIVONGOLA
248	JUSELE MIHIGO		F	"
249	JOSEPHINE WATUTA		F	"
250	JOSEPHINA ONGE MBALA	3mths	F	BANGWE
251	JACQUES ONGHE	37y.o.	m	
252	JEAN PIERRE MIRENGE KASONGO	3y.o.	M	KATUTA
253	JACQUELINE FANGO	18y.o.	F	KASHEKE
254	JULES		M	CITE ll/MBOKO
25-5	JEAN-MARIE CHILA	1y.o.	M	KAHAMA
256	JEANNETTE MUFAUME	43y.o.	F	NGALULA
257	JEANNE BAHIYE	40y.o.	F	"
258	JOSEPHINE NDOHI		F	KAMBA
259	JOSEPHINE LUNGWE		F	"
260	JUJU BUKUMBA		F	"
261	JAQUELINA MUTOCHA		F	"
262	JAQUES SUNGULA		m	"
263	KISHIBISAHA MALIANI		M	MAKOBOLAI
264	KAI		m	"
265	KABWANA BULENGE		m	"
266	KABIBI BULENGE		F	"
267	KYAKUNA KAMNOBE		F	"
267	KITABO KITAMALA		m	"
268	KAYUYA MALIYANI		m	"
269	KITUNGANO KATITA		m	"
270	KYOYO (M. NAKITUMBA's wife)		F	KATUTA
271	KIPANZA SALEHE		m	MIKUNGA
272	KALUTA MAHOKA WELONGO		M	BANGWE
273	KAGESURU FURAHISHA		F	"
274	KATAINA MMUMENGAKOBE		F	KAHAMA
275	KISE AKYENA		m	"

276	KITUMAINI ISHEKELA		m	KAHAMA
277	KABABWA WAKYENYA		m	"
278	KYOBA MBILIZI		m	"
279.	KISLE BWAMI		m	"
280	KAZUZU WETU		M	NGALULA
281	KITUNGANO USENI		M	MUKWZEI
282	KALUTA -		F	KAMBA
283	KAS I BA -		F	ILAKALA
284	KASUKU-		m	"
285	KASHIMBO MWATUMO		F	"
286	KOLETA OSENI	32y.o.	F	BANGWE
287	KAMNO MYAYO	3y.o.	M	MIKUNGA
288	KIMBITI MILUNGA	38y.o.	m	"
289	KABITI KATIIGUTA	2y.o.	F	KATUTA
290	KADOGO YOMBE	2y.o.	M	KATUTA
291	KATERANYA (Burundian Refugee)		M	BASHILUBAN DA/MBOKO
292	KASIBA KATUMBI	30y.o.	F	MUNENE
293	KISEKEDI LOTOELO	16y.o.	M	KAHAMA
294	KULIYE SHABANI	65y.o.	M	NGALULA
295	KAMPE MMJOMBO	-	M	NGAMBA
296	KEYO SUNGULA	-	m	"
297	KASHINDI SUNGULA	-	m	"
298	KALYAMTU MAKOBOLA	-	m	"
299	KAMBEMBA ASSUMANI	-	m	"
300	LUNGA JOSEPHINE	-	F	KATUTA
301	LOKOLE LUSUNGU	-	M	MIKUNGA
302	LUKANGYELA EKYAMBA	-	m	"
303	LUPONDA ESOWA	-	m	"
304	LEA SALIMA	-	F	"
305	LUKAMBELO UWANDJA	-	m	"
306	LALIA AMEMBE	-	F	"
307	LUMUMBA NDAHAZA	-	M	KAHAMA
308	LAINI MMDAMA	-	F	"
309	LUTUMBU BYAMUNGU	-	m	"
310	LUSHI MWASHITI	-	F	NGALULA
311	LENDEZA MNANDOTO	-	F	ILAKALA
312	LALIA MWA'A	3y.o.	F	MIKUNGA
313	KAMPE MULENDA		M	NGAMBA
314	LOKELE TSHILANGO	83y.o.	M	MIKUNGA
315	LOKALELO MMANDA	70y.o.	m	"
316	LUNYEMBA ABEKYA	26y.o.	m	"
317	LALIA EMBETE'	:3y.o.	F	"
318	LOKOLE TABISENGWA	8y.o.	F	"
319	LIPANGA BARUTI	3y.o.	M	KATUTA
320	LEKUMU		m	"
321	LAHELINYASSA	39y.o.	F	KASHEKEZI
322	LYAENDA MNOBE	7y.o.	M	KAHAMA
323	LWANGELA HAMISI	11y.o.	M-	"

324	LWAMBO MBILIZI	8mths	m	KAHAMA
325	MUSEMEWA (M. KINEKA's wife)		F	MAKOBOLAI
326	Mr. KINEKA's Mother	-	F	"
327.	MALIANI GODEFROIE (Segorn)	-	m	"
328	MAPWATA MALIAN I	-	m	"
329	MARIE NALUSHUMBA	-	F	"
330	MATESO	-	F	"
331	MIMA	-	F	"
332	MUSUNGU BULENGE	-	m	"
333	MUGANGANE WA BAZIBA	-	m	"
334	MUBANGUBANGU	-	m	"
335	MALOLA ASSUMANI	-	m	"
336	MANA (Mr. KANGERE's wife)	-	F	"
337	MULILIKWA BUGARAMA	-	m	"
338	MAUWA ROSA			"
339	MASASIWENYA		M	MIKUNGA
340	MAKOMA CHRISTINE		F	"
341	MWENGE NABAUKYAKA		F	"
342	MANDELENI LWABABA		F	"
343	MILINGANYO ALONDAMWAMI	-	m	"
344	MULISHO SHUKURU	-	m	"
345	MLONDONI KACHELEWA	-	m	"
346	MLASHI MIYAMBANO	-	F	"
347	MAWAZO SALIMA	-	F	"
348	MKYUNGU FUMORO	-	M	BANGWE
349	NZALIWA HOSHINAWAKE	-	M	"
350	MAHONECHO ONGEMBALA MWEC	-	F	"
351	MLASHI ONGEMBALAMWECI	-	F	"
352	MANDELENI SALUMU	-	F	"
353	MAENOSHO SALUMU TAMBE	-	m	"
354	MMBUNDA ODENI	-	m	"
355	MAYA ODENI	-	m	"
356	MWENDA MLUBI	-	F	"
357	MAAO SALUMU	-	m	"
358	MMANDAMA EMANGA	-	M	KAHAMA
359	MAZAMBI KYALONDAWA	-	m	"
360	MELANIYA LOTOELO	-	F	"
361	NTEMA LOTOELO	-	M	KAHAMA
362	MBUMBA LOTOELO	-	m	"
363	MINYEKO AKYENA	-	M	"
.364	MMBOMBA AKYENA	-	m	"
365	MALENGA YELAMWA	-	F	"
366	MALUMBE MMDAMA	-	m	"
367	MASHAKA MMDAMA	-	m	"
368	MARIMU MAZAMBI	-	F	"
369	MSAFIRI ABWAKE	-	m	"
370	MWENDA MBILIZI	-	m	"
371	MAUWA ASAN I	-	F	NGALULA

372	MAKALA ILANGIYE		M	NGALULA
373	NSOMBWA TAMUSAALE		F	"
374	MBELECIHERI		F	"
375	MBELECI MAKYAMBE FEZA		F	"
376	MORTON BENGA		M	"
377	MINYEKO ISHIBABU		M	"
378	MWALIMU AMBILO		M	MUKWEZI
379	MOMBO AKAMBA	-	M	LUSAMBO
380	MAUWA	-	F	MUNENE
381	MUKE MASTA	-	F	"
382	MUBANGU BANGU	-	M	"
383	MWENGE ABEYA-EKA	-	F	KASHEKE
384	MIMA NA-ABUE	-	F	"
385	MANDELI NABITO	-	F	KIVONGOLWA
386	MLONDA EBUKA	-	M	KAMBA
387	MKYUNGU EKYELA (EKELA)	-	M.	"
388	MMBUMDA SALEM	-	M	"
389	MAYA -	-	F	"
390	MIYUNGANYA POLIDIRE	-	F	KASHEKEZI
391	MIRENGE BARUTI	-	M	"
392	MASUMBUKO BARUTI	-	M	"
393	MALOBA BARUTI	-	M	"
394	MAKWATA GODET	-	F	"
395	MILONDANI -		F	"
396	MAPE NDO -		F	"
397	MLASI NAMINYEKO		F	"
398	MUTOTO FRANQOIS		M	"
399	MAZAMANI MMENENE		M	"
400	MUSUNGU WEKELA		M	"
401	MARIA + 1 SON		F	"
402	MBIRIMA EMMANUEL	30y.o.	M	KIVONGOLWA
403	MAHONESHO WAMULOLA	65y.o.	F	"
404	MARIABO NABAJUMBI	59y.o.	F	KALOMO
405	MUGANGANE ROGER	57y.o.	M	KALOMO
406	MAONESHO BILEMO	57y.o.	F	"
407	MALIPO BENI		F	"
408	MANDE SALUMU		F	"
409	MARIA NYALUSHUMBA-	52y.o.	F	KANYANGWE
410	MAVUNDJA ECLESIA		M	ILAKALA
411	MAESA KAKUMBU		F	"
412	M'KYUNGU W'EKELA	24y.o.	M	BANGWE
413	MWANYI MALENGELA	45y.o.	M	"
414	MASEMO MUTAMBALA	10mths	M	"
415	MAMAN FATUMA		F	MIKUNGA
416	MUSHO ELOCO	3y.o.	M	"
417	MOTEMA ELOCO	5mths	M	"
418	MWEN'ESUBE ELOCO	75y.o.	M	MIKUNGA
419	MILENGANI ALONDAWA	55y.o.	M	MIKUNGA

420	MLONDANI MANYINWA	21y.o.	M	MIKUNGA
421	MITANGA HOMARI	I an	F	"
422	MWA'A ABEKYA	43y.o.	M	"
423	MAOMBI JEANO	6y.o.	F	"
424	MIKABOKABO 101	13y.o.	M	"
425	MAWAZO SELEMANI	49y.o.	F	"
426	MMENENWA LUSAKANYA	14y.o.	M	"
427	MASOKA ABEKYA	5y.o.	F	"
428	MMBANGO LUANGA	11y.o.	M	KATUTA
429	MIRENGE BAHATI	40y.o.	F	"
430	MIHIGO BARUTI	18y.o.	M	"
431	MITOMBO BARUTI	9y.o.	M	"
432	MACOZI MIRENGE KASONGO	9y.o.	F	"
433	MASUMBUKO LABWIKA	28y.o.	M	"
434	MWASHANBA JOMBE	4y.o.	F	"
435	MALENGA MMSSA	7y.o.	F	"
436	MUKUNIKINI TOSHA	6y.o.-	F	"
437	MALEKANI SUMAHILI	4y.o.	M	"
438	MMONGA EHANGO	29y.o.	M	"
439	MUSA LUMINA	14y.o.	M	"
440	MALENGA PUPA	9y.o.	F	"
441	MAPWATA PUPA	13y.o.	M	"
442	MAWAZO PUPA	2y.o.	F	"
443	MARIAMU KISIMBA	7y.o.	F	KASHEKEZI
444	MOSHICHAMLUNGU	14y.o.	F	"
445	MAMBOLEO WILONDJA	79y.o.	M	"
446	MUSAFIRI ABEKYAMWALI	61y.o.	M	"
447	MWENELWATA LUKABA	16y.o.	M	"
448	MBELECIABALE	11y.o.	M	"
449	MALENGA BI'ANGWA	31y.o.	F	
450	MBEUMU ETANDO	10y.o.	M	KASHEKI
451	MUNOKO	-	M	KABUMBE
452	MU'OSA	-	M	"
453	MWALIMU AMBELA	-	M	MUKWEZI
454	MAYANGA ISHIBATWA	-	M	LUSAMBO
455	MAMBO-	-	M	
456	MARIE -	-	F	MUKANDJAKO U
457	MUKELA -	-	M	CITE III MBOKC
458	MINEBWE SHIABWE	27y.o.	M	MUNENE
459	MAETA MUFAUME	14y.o.	M	"
460	MUFANDJALA TUBEREZA	39y.o.	M	"
461	MACOZI ABWE	8mths		"
462	MIRENGE NGAVANWA		F	KAHAMA
463	M'MGI ENOKE		F	"
464	MMONGAPOPO	6y.o.	M	"
65	MWENE LUKU SHILA	70y.o.	M	"
466	MUTAMBALA CHAMLUNGU	14y.o.	M	"
467	MUSAFIRI LOTENGYA	8y.o.	M	

468	MWASHITE ETABO	11y.o.	F	NGALULA
469	MINYEKO BYASSONGA	25y.o.	M	"
470	MWANGAZA LUBENOA	66y.o.	F	"
471	MAIVUNO NAMUSEANGWA	35y.o.	F	"
472	MAONESHO LUNGWE		F	KAMBA
473	MLASHI MAYAMBE		F	"
474	MLASHI LOKELELO	-	F	"
475	MAPENDO MASAMBA	-	F	"
476	MATOMBO ALIMASI	-	m	"
477	MWALIBOLA BUSUNGU	-	F	"
478	MBAYA BURISENGE	-	F	"
479	WEE EBELETE	-	F	"
480	MWASHITI RUHINOIZA	-	F	"
481	MUIBA KECHA BARUAMI	-	F	"
482	MARIA ASSAN I	-	F	"
483	MWASHITE NALUSHENGE	-	F	"
484	MUSUKIWA NANDOLANI	-	F	"
485	MALENGA TOTO	-	F	"
486	MATENDO RUHAYA	-	m	"
487	NDAMA RUSANGIZA (DELPHIN) Deacon	-	M	MAKOBOLAI
488	NESHO MIKOMO	-	m	"
489	NYIHASHA MAMAKAMANGO	-	M	MAKOBOLAI
490	NAKASHINDI	-	F	KATUTA
491	NYASSA ASAMBA	-	F	MIKUNGA
492	NYOTA KIBISWA	-	F	MIKUNGA
493	NAMTMUDACHI ESOA	-	m	"
494	NAKESENGE MWAMINI	-	F	"
495	NALUPONDA MISUNGA	-	F	"
496	NAMATE CHABENGANA	-	F	"
497	NYOTA EN DAN I	-	F	"
498	NAAMBACHA ITONGWA	-	F	"
499	NAMBULECHIBWA NGUBULWA	-	F	"
500	NABEMBA NISALO ONGE	-	F	"
501	NATANI SILA	-	M	KAHAMA
502	NYENGELA BWAMI	-	m	"
503	NYENGELA MLASI	-	F	KAHAMA
504	NAMIRENGE NGANYWA	-	F	"
505	NAGAYONE NDAHAZA	-	F	"
506	NYAMBWE MMDAMA	-	m	"
507	NYOTA MBILIZI	-	F	NGALULA
508	NAGUNGU BUKUMBA	-	F	"
509	NAGUNGU ABWE	-	F	"
510	NAGUNGU ANNA	-	F	"
511	NAGUNGU THERESE	-	F	"
512	NAABWE LOHI	-	F	"
513	NAMIYA RAMAZANI	-	m	"
514	NAMBWELA SOPHIE	-	F	KASHEKEZI

515	NAMALELEMBE MWAMINI		F	KASHEKEZI
516	NYANGYE LUKANGAKYE		M	KAMBA
517	NANTHANIE SHILA		M	KALUMO
518	NAWELONGO IVONNE		F	KASHEKEZI
519	NYOTA ITONGWA		F	"
519	NABYOCHUCHWA		m	"
520	NAMWATUMU		M	"
521	NDAHILONGO RASHIDI	52y.o.	M	KIVONGOLWA
522	NYASSA OMAR		F	KALOMO
523	NANWARI KARINGINGO		F	KANYAGWE
524	NANGOME JULINE	40y.o.	F	"
525	NDA'ALA FILS DE MUYENGA	3mths	m	"
526	NAPINDA KUNGU		F	ILAKALA
527	NAWELONGO LEYA		F	BANGWE
528	NAYASSA MPENDA	38y.o.	F	MIKUNGA
529	NYOTA ELOCO	Ian	F	MIKUNGA
530	NAMSENGELO MAYALIWA	23y.o.	F	"
531	NAMTE OMARI	5y.o.	F	"
534	NAYOTA YONASI	51y.o.	F	"
535	NYASA NABILUBI	43y.o.	F	"
536	NABYTUNGA NAMWEMBE	60y.o.	F	"
537	NALMLELWA	57y.o.	F	"
538	NGYUKU OREDI	3y.o.	F	"
539	NAMABAMBA MIGUNGA	73y.o.	F	"
540	NALWAMBA NAYENGA	67y.o.	F	"
541	NAKAMANA NYIHASHA	48y.o.	F	KATUTA
542	NANYOKU NGALULA	70y.o.	F	"
543	NALOEBO N'EBUNDA	3y.o.	F	"
544	NAMWASHA KIRENGE	Ian	F	"
545	NANGENDO MUHERONA	5y.o.	F	"
546	NJONJO APENDEKI	2y.o.	F	MUNENE
547	NISIMO NAPENDA	80y.o.	F	"
548	NATABU APENDEKI	56y.o.	F	KAHAMA
549	NAMMENGA MENGWA	60y.o.	M	NGALULA
550	NAKYOYO NAKITUMBA	-	F	KAMBA
551	NAMINYEKU LWENDO	-		KAMBA
552	NEEMA MAYAYA	-		KAMBA
553	NDALA MBILIZI	-		KAMBA
554	NDAHO BUMENGE	-		KAMBA
555	NEEMAISHARA			"
556	OLOMWENE ISA		M	NGALULA
557	ONGA OBE CLAUDE	17y.o.	M	KASHEKEZI
558	OMBENI JIMMY		M	KAMBA
559	PATRICK KONGOLO		M	IKUNGA
560	PENDEZA ABANGWA		F	KAHAMA
561	PENDEZA ISA		F	NGALULA
562	PATILI MIHIGO		M	NGALULA
563	PADRI SUKARI MIRENGE KASONGO	15y.o.	M	KATUTA

564	PRIMO SWEDI	43y.o.	M	KATUTA
565	PETELO LWE'YA	-	M	KAMBA
566	REMY MALIANI	-	M	MAKOBOLAI
567	REHEMA APOLINA	-	F	MIKUNGA
568	REHEMA ACHAI	-	F	BANGWE
569	RIZIKI ODENI	-	F	BANGWE
570	REHEMA NAMBWELA	-	F	BANGWE
571	RAZARO	-	M	KASHEKEZI
572	RIZIKI GODET	-	F	KASHEKEZI
573	RAZARO LWAMESO	-	M	BANGWE
574	RAMAZANI MIRAMBA	18y.o.	M	MIKUNGA
575	ROSA ECHA	10mth	F	MIKUNGA
576	REHEMA ABEKYA	6y.o.	F	MIKUNGA
577	REHEMA MUSEMBWA	11y.o.	F	MIKUNGA
578	RWAKANA NGUBANA	40y.o.	M	MUNENE
579	RUNYURIZI RUBARUBA		M	KAMBA
580	RAMAZANI ESUBE		M	KAMBA
581	RAJABU LWENDO	-	M	KAMBA
582	ROSA ZABIBU	-	F	KAMBA
583	SENGE GODELIVE	-	F	KATUTA
584	SWEDI AMISI	-	M	MIKUNGA
585	SHOLA MARTA ELONGO	-	F	MIKUNGA
586	SAFI NACHIBIYA	-	F	MIKUNGA
587	SAMSON MANONO	-	M	MIKUNGA
588	SAFI NACHIBIYA	-	F	MIKUNGA
589	SAMSON MANONO	-	M	BA NGWE
590	SAFO WABANGWA	-	M	BANGWE
591	SUNGULA MMALE	-	M	BANGWE
592	SAMUEL ONGE MBALAMWECHI	-	F	KAHAMA
593	SUMBUNI SAFARI MBALAMWECHI	-	F	KAHAMA
594	SIKITIKO EMBWE	-	M	KAHAMA
595	SAFILOTOELO	-	M	KAHAMA
596	SHUKURU LOTOELO	-	F	KAHAMA
597	SUNGULA WACHAULE	-	M	KAHAMA
598	SABITI ICHEKALA	-	M	KAHAMA
599	SIUZIKI MBILIZI	-	M	KAHAMA
600	SITUAI ABULE	-	M	LUSAMBO
601	SHAURIAPUTULA	-	M	KASHEKEZI
602	SAVERI LWAMBANYA	-	M	KIVONGOLWA
603	SAVERI LWAMBANYA	-	F	KASENYA
604	SHIBAKE ECHA	-	F	KASHEKEZI
605	SHEMEDI MAHUNGU	-	M	KASHEKEZI
606	SALOME MAKUMBA	-	F	KASHEKEZI
608	SALIA NAMAHEMBA	8mths	F	KALOMO
609	SHAONA MIHIGO		F	ILAKALA
610	SHAPATA MIRENGE	35y.o.	M	BANGWE
611	SIYAWEZI MUGANGANI	26y.o.	M	BANGWE
612	SAFI WABUCHIBWA	4y.o.	M	BANGWE

613	SHANGWE ASSUMANI	60y.o.	M	BANGWE
614	SWEDI ALIMASI	-	M	BANGWE
615	SADI ALUMBE	1y.o.	F	MIKUNGA
616	SELAMANI LUMUNGA	50y.o.	F	MIKUNGA
618	SUNGULA AOMBE	49y.o.	F	MIKUNGA
619	SAFI ELOCHO	8y.o.	M	MIKUNGA
620	SALIYA NAMAHEMBA	9y.o.	M	KATUTA
621	SAKINA MIRAMBA	3y.o.	F	KATUTA
622	SANGANI RUKAMBO	31y.o.	F	KATUTA
623	SALUMU EMBETE	13y.o.	M	KATUTA
624	SANGO MATO MUKALO	1y.o.	F	KATUTA
625	SHIAPA BARUTI	10y.o.	M	KATUTA
626	SAIDI MIRENGE KASONGO	67y.o.	M	KASHEKEZI
627	SAKINA SOFIA MIRENGE KASONGO	3y.o.	M	KASHEKEZI
627	SAFARIMBEKE	13y.o.	F	KASHEKEZI
628	SAMALENGE MYENGE	12y.o.	F	KASHEKEZI
629	SANGO ELO'CHO	14y.o.	F	KAHAMA
630	SUZANNE ALONDA	35y.o.	M	KAHAMA
631	SAFI MUTEREKWA	-	F	KAMBA
632	SALIMA AVOMBA	-	M	KAMBA
633	SANGO HONORINE	-	F	KAMBA
634	SHIMO SHILA	-	M	MAKOBOLA1
635	SOFIA GERARD	-	F	MIKUNGA
636	SWEDI RAMAZANI	-	F	BANGWE
637	SOFIA CHABANI	-	F	BANGWE
638	TUBEREZA CHABANI	-	F	BANGWE
639	TABI SENGO SALIMA	-	F	KASHEKEZI
640	TATU ODENI	58y.o.	M	KANYAGWE
641	TENGESHA NSASECHA		F	BANGWE
642	THERESE BOBILYA	2y.o.	F	MIKUNGA
643	TONGYE HALI	6y.o.	F	KASHEKEZI
644	TINOA SAIDI	8y.o.	F	KASHEKEZI
645	TENGENESHA BIBIHERI	74y.o.	M	MUNENE
646	TOSHA AMIDO	7y.o.	F	MUNENE
647	TOBONGYE APENDEKI	72y.o.	M	NGALULA
648	TELESYA LEON	-	M	KAMBA
649	TUBEREZ MASHAKO	-	F	KAMBA
650	TATU BYAMUNGU	-	F	KAMBA
651	TAMBWE MULENJWE	-	M	MIKUNGA
652	TEKETEKE RAMAZANI	-	F	KAHAMA
653	TOSHA KABEMBA	9y.o.	M	MIKUNGA
654	TERESYA NANGELEI		M	MIKUNGA
655	USURIWENYA	5y.o.	F	KATUTA
656	UNGWA MMDAMA	8mths	M	MUNENE
657	UMBELECHA ABEKYA	-	F	KAMBA
658	UNGWA PAUL	-	F	MIKUNGA
659	VUMIPUPA	-	M	MIKUNGA
660	VINCENT KITUNGANO	-	M	KAHAMA

661	VICTORINE STELA		M	KAHAMA
662	WABIKWA KAHINDO	-	M	KAHAMA
663	WENYA AMISI	-	M	KAHAMA
664	WAMAKANDA ESUBE	-	F	KAHAMA
665	WILONDJA LISASI	-	M	KAHAMA
666	WALUMONA SADI	-	M	KAMBA
667	WABO MBILIZI	-	M	KAMBA
668	WALUCHWELA MBILIZI	31y.o.	M	MIKUNGA
669	WALUMONA MBILIZI	10y.o.	M	MIKUNGA
670	WANYATA AMISI	12y.o.	M	MIKUNGA
671	WEELENDA AMISI	1y.o.	M	KATUTA
672	WATUNGYA HAUBELE	9y.o.	F	KASHEKEZI
673	WILONDJA JANO	16y.o.	M	MUNENE
674	WEBUNGA LUSAKANYA	18y.o.	F	NGALULA
675	WEBALO NGOMBE	13y.o.	M	NGALULA
676	WABALA MLASHI	-	F	KAMBA
677	WELONGO SAID[		F	MIKUNGA
678	KAMAKANDA WAESUBE	-	F	MIKUNGA
679	WILONDJA WAESUBE	-	F	KAHAMA
680	WITU ANGELE	-	F	KAHAMA
681	YOSTINA LOPONGA	-	F	KASHEKEZI
682	YENA APENDEKI	-	F	KASHEKEZI
683	YENA NAKALA	-	M	KASENYA
684	YALUNDAWA NGYELA	-	M	KAMBA
685	YOHALI EVELINA	-	F	KALOMO
686	YANGWA MISA	-	F	BANGWE
687	YOHANA NALWAGE	60y.o.	F	MIKUNGA
688	YOSHUA MALEANI	40y.o.	M	MIKUNGA
689	YUSTANI BULENGE	27y.o.	F	MIKUNGA
690	YOSE BULENGE	8y.o.	M	KATUTA
691	YENA NAMWANUE	20y.o.	F	KATUTA
692	YOHANA MWAKWA	11y.o.	F	KASHEKEZI
693	YUNIKI NISHIMO	40y.o.	F	KASHEKEZI
694	YOHANA GERARD	1y.o.	F	KASHEKEZI
695	YENEZA LUMINA	17y.o.	F	KASHEKEZI
696	YOHA NA'YENGE	1y.o.	M	KASHEKEZI
697	YELAMWA ELISHA	-	M	MUKWEZI
698	YOSE MAONYESHO	-	F	MAKOBOLA1
699	YOKI MAANGAIKO	-	F	MIKUNGA
700	YOHANA OBEDI	-	F	NGALULA
701	YOSEPFU OBEDI	1y.o.	F	MIKUNGA
702	ZENEA OBEDI	1y.o.	F	KASHEKEZI
703	ZALIYA NAMAHEMBA		M	KABUMBE
704	ZAINA NYAMBWE		F	KAMBA
705	ZAWADI ABEKYA		F	KATUTA
706	ZAINA ATEMBO	1y.o.	F	KASHEKEZI
707	ZABULONI ATEMBO		M	KABUMBE
708	ZABIBU ONGWA		F	KAMBA

709 1 FAILA ANGENYELE F I KATUTA

NOTE: 709 persons + 109 members (of family cited but) not identified = **818 PERSONS KILLED AT MAKOBOLA**

B. TABLE No 2 (SUMMARY)

	VILLAGES CONCERNED	MALES KILLED	FEMALES	TTL
1	BANGWE	36	30	66
2.	BASHILLIBANDA MBOKO	01	00	01
3.	CITE 11 MBOKO	01	00	01
4.	CITE III MBOKO	01	00	01
5.	ILAKALA	03	06	09
6.	KATUTA	24	29	53
7.	KAHAMA	66	40	106
8.	KABUMBE	04	00	04
9.	KASHEKEZI	46	36	82
10.	KASENYA	01	03	04
11.	KAMBA	43	38	81
12.	KALOMO	07	09	16
13.	KANYAGWE	02	03	05
14.	KABONDOZI MBOKO	04	00	04
15.	kIVONGOLWA	05	06	11
16.	LUSAMBO	04	00	04
17.	MAKOBOLAI	20	18	38
18.	MIKUNGA	60	70	130
19.	MUKWEZI	09	00	09
20.	MUNENE	09	10	19
21.	MBOKO	19	00	19
22	MUKANJAKALO	00	01	01
23	NGALULA	130	24	154
TOTALS		495	323	818

II. 2. OTHER KILLINGS THAT TOOK PLACE IN SOUTH KIVU

Period from January to February 1999

NUMBER		NAME	VILLAGE / LOCALITY
	1.	Mr. RUBANGO	CHIBEKE - BURHALE WALUNGU
	2.	Mr. CHISHUGI	LUBONA / WALUNGU
	3.	Mr. MULUMEODERHWA	CHIBANDA-BURHALE/WALUNGU
	4.	Mr. LWABOSHI	BURHALE Center / WALUNGU
	5.	Mr. Perroquet	BURHALE Center / WALUNGU
	6.	Mr. BAKUNZI (old shepherd of the village)	LUBONA / WALUNGU

7.	Aide - chauffeur de Mr.	BUTILIZA / WALUNGU	
	TEMBO		
8-	Mr. BISIMWA	BUTILIZA / WALUNGU	
9.	An unidentified young businessman	BUTILIZA Center / WALUNGU	
15.	Six merchants from lkoma, on their	BURHALE / WALUNGU	
	Way to MWENGA, killed at		
16.	A woman of MASHANGO	BUTUZA / WALUNGU	
	BURHALE		
17.	Mr. Bosco CHISHUGI	LUBONA I WALUNGU	
18	Mr. Bosco NAMAHIRA	LUBONA / WALUNGU	
19.	Mr. MWALIMU CHIREGE	LUBONA / WALUNGU	
22.	Three persons from BUKAVU	MASHANGO - BURHALE WALUNGU	
	(Beaten, then killed)		
30.	Eight unidentified persons whose	NSHESHA WALUNGU	
	Bodies were found drowned in		
	The river NSHESHA		
31.	Mr. OLINABANJI CHIREGE	LUBONA / WALUNGU	
32.	Mr. Nestor CHIKUJU	LUBONA I WALUNGU	
	(Chief of IRABATA 's plantations)		
33.	Mr. Oscar MUSHEMBE	LUBONA / WALUNGU	
34.	Mr. CHIREMA KALABA	LUBONA / WALUNGU	
35.	Mr. ZAHINDA	LUBONA / WALUNGU	
36.	Mr. C6lestin MUGUNDA	CHIHERANO / WALUNGU	
37.	Mr. MATABA CHEHU	CHIHERANO / WALUNGU	
38.	Mr. KASIKA Modeste	CHIHERANO / WALUNGU	
39.	Mr. KAMANYU CHIDAHA	MULAMBA / WALUNGU	
40.	Mr. MPANGIRWA	MULAMBA I WALUNGU	
41.	Mme. MPANGIRWA	MULAMBA / WALUNGU	
43.	Two sons of Mr. NTUMULO	MUSHINGA / WALUNGU	
45.	Two persons whose identities	CHIHERANO / WALUNGU	
	Could not be determined		

MEN ARE SHOT WITH NO QUESTIONS ASKED

1. RUBANGO, of the town of Chibeke in the Burhale/Walungu region;
2. Mr. CHISHUGI, of the town of Lubona in the Walungu region;
3. Mr. MULUMEODERHWA, of the town of Chibonda in the Burhale/Walungu region;
4. Mr. LUABOSHI, of the town of Centre-Burhale;
5. Mr. PERROQUET, of the town of Centre-Burhale;
6. Mr. BAKUNZI, an elderly shepherd of the town of Lubona in the Walungu region;
7. Mr. BISIMWA, of the town of Bututza

Beside the above-named victims, numerous civilians are killed anywhere they encounter the invading Rwandan-Burundian-Ugandan military forces. Those who are killed far away from their hometown are not identified, because everything is taken away from them.

This was the case for
    a. A young merchant killed in the center of the town of Butuza;
    b. Six (6) merchants from the town of Ikoma, en route to the town of Urega, killed in the town of Burhale.
    c. Three (3) persons from Bukavu, beaten, robbed, and killed in the town of Mashango.

MASSACRE OF 300 PEOPLE BY BURUNDIAN-RWAN-DAN-UGANDAN FORCES, IN THE TOWN OF KATOGOTA

The killing of Congolese people does not need to reach the millions before the Western world shows outrage. Nevertheless, the count continues mounting and the developed world, especially America and Western Europe show no outrage, there is a muted response from the so-called lands of liberty and democracy. There is no urgency to stop these crimes.

Many of the atrocities being committed in the Congo are not known, because, in order for their crimes not to be uncovered, the invading forces kill everyone in the town, children, women, the elderly, the sick, and the disabled. Then they burn down the entire town.

This fate was visited upon the town of KATOGOTA. If this massacre came to be known, investigated, and confirmed, it was because a survivor escaped the systematic killing perpetrated by these invading forces.

The town of Katogota is located about 35 miles (60 km) south of Bukavu.

The missionary agency, MISNA, a catholic news agency, reported out of Rome on May 20th, 2000, that the "victims were either shot or hacked to death with machetes." Indeed, the Rwandan-Uganda-Burundian are expert in the techniques of hacking to death, with machetes, children, women, the elderly, and the helpless. Who can forget the television scenes, in 1994, of Rwandans hacking other Rwandans to death. Now the Rwandans have carried this sordid expertise into the Congo territory and are putting to practice on the Congolese.

And America and Europe sit, watch, and let it go on.

This massacre in Katogota took place during one night, that of May 14-15, 2000.

The lone survivor of this confirmed massacre told the investigators and MISNA what and how it happened:

"When it got dark the massacre began...It lasted from 7:30 in the evening to around 5:00 on Monday morning. The bodies were first dispersed in a large area in and around the village and then either dragged to the river and thrown in the water."

What is it going to take for America and Europe, who are paying Rwanda, Burundi, and Uganda to kill Congolese, what is it going to take for them to ask these murderers to stop and go back to their respective countries?

5

Mutilated Children

The Rwandan-Ugandan-Burundian forces do not hesitate to mutilate children, for any excuse that they may find. Furthermore, any child who refuses to carry out any given task, no matter how risky it may be, runs the risk of facing either mutilation or death.

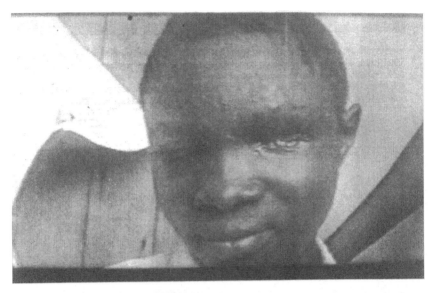

Are these atrocities lesser than the ones committed in Kosovo or in Serbia? Why then are American and European governments still financing Uganda-Burundi-Rwandan invasion and occupation of the Congo by financially and militarily aiding these three countries?

A 13 YEAR-OLD GIRL ESCAPED FROM BEING BURNED ALIVE

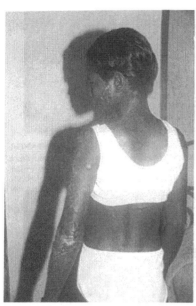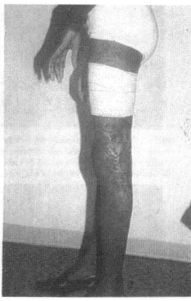

During the massacres perpetrated by Ugandan-Rwandan soldiers in the town of Kasala, in the north of Katanga on the night of 27th to 28th of June, 1999, men, women, and children were locked up into huts that were then set afire. Over 40 people died in this manner. The 13 year-old, Miss. MUJINGA WA BANZA escaped from this fire execution with burns all over her body.

Is this a lesser atrocity than the ones committed in Kosovo or in Serbia? Is a black life worth less than a white life? Why then are American and European governments still financing Uganda-Burundi-Rwandan invasion and occupation of the Congo by financially and militarily aiding these three countries?

6

Raped Women Who Lived to Tell Their Stories

In this war, because of the way the customs view rape, when women are raped, they are so ashamed that they do not tell anybody else what happened to them, not only because of the shame this brings to them and their families, and their bodies being defiled, but also because they fear that no other man (their husbands, or any other men) would want to be with them afterwards.

So, the following cases are just the tip of the iceberg, when considering the numbers of women and little Congolese girls who are raped on a daily basis, in the Rwandan-Burundian-Ugandan occupied territories.

These 10 women were raped by Rwandan soldiers when they moved in their town, Musanjie, about 12 km from Kabinda. They are,

- MWISSANGE KAYAYA (19 years old);
- KASONGO KASONGO (19 years old);
- MOBESHE LUKUEKA (45 years old);
- NTUMBA KASONGO (35 years old);
- TSHITA SAPU (60 years old);
- LUMANU KASONGO (33 years old);
- EPINDU KALOBO (20 years old);
- NGOYI NSOMWE (32 years old);
- SHALA MALANGU (21 years old);
- BINIENGE TSHIKUDI (20 years old).

Are these atrocities lesser than the ones committed in Kosovo or in Serbia? Why then are American and European governments still financing Uganda-Burundi-Rwandan invasion and occupation of the Congo by financially and militarily aiding these three countries?

INDIVIDUAL STORIES:

Mrs. LUMANU KASONGO (33 years old)

Mrs. LUMANU KASONGO, of the town of Musanjie near Kabinda was raped by up to ten Rwandan soldiers, when they invaded and took over her hometown. Even though she had a small child that she was caring for, the Rwandan soldiers did not care, they repeatedly raped her.

MRS. MOBESHE LUKUEKA (Born in 1954, mother to 9 children: 2 girls, 7 boys)

IN HER OWN WORDS: "Myself, when the Rwandan soldiers arrested me, they took me behind the little house and I saw the other women being taken into the bush. One woman with about twenty Rwandan soldiers. And there were at least ten groups since there were about ten women. Personally, I was beaten at first, then tortured, because I had slapped one of the Rwandan soldiers.

"Afterwards, I was tied with ropes like a pig, and soldiers of my sons' age raped me repeatedly.

"At my age, I could not stand being raped repeatedly by several men, so my genitals gave way. I was bleeding like a faucet. In spite of the blood, they kept raping me. Then toward 5 PM, they ordered me to go back to my hometown otherwise they were going to kill me. I could not walk so I crawled on all four, naked, until I got to where Congolese and Zimbabwean soldiers were. They took me to be treated at the MONUC (the United Nations monitors). After this event, my husband chased me out of our house because I had been raped. Today, my children have been abandoned without their mother."

MISS SHALA MALANGU (Born in 1978, State Diploma with a major in Education (Pedagogy) from the Kabinda Institute)

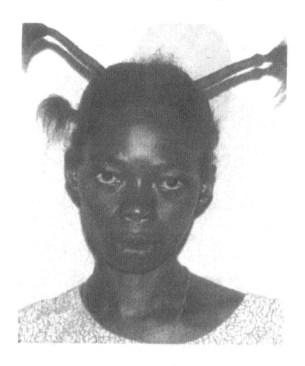

IN HER OWN WORDS: "I was arrested about 12 km from Kabinda, with my sac of fufu I had bought for my parents. They took everything that I had and they threw me in the bush. Five Rwandan soldiers followed me and raped me repeatedly. Then, they chased us in the forest. Myself, I ran naked on all four until I arrived at about 5 km from Kabinda, where Congolese soldiers carried me to the hospital. I spent 3 days in the hospital."

MRS. NGOY NSOMWE (Born in 1966. Married and has six children. The last child was 1 year and three months old, when she was raped).

IN HER OWN WORDS: "It was November 25, 1999 that I was kidnapped about 35 km from Kabinda. I had gone to the fields to get cassava (manioc) for food for my children and my husband. On our way back, we were rounded up by Rwandan soldiers, and, not far from the place, there was a small house where they took us, and where we found the Rwandan soldiers' commandant. Right in the middle of the forest.

"One of the soldiers took me by the hand and asked me to go and show him where the Congolese soldiers were. Because I refused, he led me into the commandant's house, where I saw several members of our Kabinda district being detained. Civilians who had gone hunting several days ago, but did not make it back, so that their families have been looking for them for several days to no-avail.

"Then I saw five soldiers come and drag me outside. They ripped my clothes off, and threw my baby into the bush. Two soldiers held me by the hands like on a cross. And they were over twenty in number, lined up in front of me, coming forth and taking their turn to rape me. I cried as loud as I could but none of them showed any pity and no one came to my rescue.

"When these twenty had finished raping me, I saw another line formed in front of me getting ready to rape me. This is when I passed out. When I woke up, I was naked and in the district of Kabinda, in front of the United Nations staff and the soldiers of the Congolese army. I could not walk any longer and I was carried to the hospital."

7

Scorched-Earth Campaign Aimed at Taking Control of Congolese Mines

In order to gain access and control over the minerals of the Congo, Rwandan, Burundian, and Ugandan forces have been practicing a scorched-earth method. They attack unarmed towns, kill and drive people away, and then burn down the entire towns. That way they can take control of the mines without anyone to contend with.

These invaders attacked the entire district of Ngweshe in the Bushi region.

The towns of Mubumbano, Lubona, Mushinga on February 16th, 1999;

All the towns along the Bwahungu route, in Tubimbi, on February 18th;

Including the town of Urega, in the Mwenga region; and the town of Kitutu on February 27th.

Finally, the Rwandan-Burundian-Ugandan forces took over the gold mines of Kamituga and Lugushwa.

Five thousand (5,000) civilians (mostly women, children, and the elderly) were massacred in this region of the South Kivu province, within the first few months of 1999.

The aim is to depopulate the entire region so that the mines are left to be exploited, and the Rwandan-Burundian-Ugandan can settle in this region, making it a de-facto Rwanda-Burundi-Ugandan territory.

8

The Rwandan Gendocide of 1994, What Does it Have to Do with the Congo?

The Rwandan genocide of 1994 was between **Rwandans** against **Rwandans.** The Tutsis are Rwandans. The Hutus are also Rwandans. Both lingual or ethnic groups have been killing each other since the Belgians, who colonized them, set one group above the other. After independence, the two groups have taken turn taking power, then using it to slaughter the other group.

The genocide in 1994 was triggered by the fact that the Rwandans shot down the plane that was bringing their own president back home. The president, then, was a Hutu: Juvenal Abyarimana. So the Hutus suspected that the Tutsis conspired and killed "their" president. So, they planned and carried out the 1994 genocide against the Tutsis, a genocide that the international community could have prevented.

The United Nations committee that investigated the shooting down of Abyarimana's plane has released a report that concluded that the person who ordered the killing of Abyarimana was Paul Kagame, a Tutsi and the head of the Rwandan army when Abyarimana, a Hutu, was president.

Now Paul Kagame has made himself president. Meaning, now the Tutsis have power in Rwanda, as in Burundi and in Uganda. So, instead of making peace with their fellow countryfolks, they have continued the cycle of co-genocide and are hunting down their fellow countrypeople, the Hutus, who have been running all over the Great Lakes.

So the West and America, feeling guilty for not stopping the 1994 genocide of Rwandans upon Rwandans, now shy from condemning the atrocities and the genocide that Tutsis of Rwanda, Burundi, and Uganda are carrying out in the Congo.

The Congo, indeed, had nothing to do with all the co-genocide that has been going on, back-and-forth, between these two groups, in these three countries.

In fact, "Security" is the code word, the excuse, and the hiding shield that is used to justify these three countries invasion of the Congo. An invasion that started out as an outright attempt to assassinate the Congolese President Laurent Kabila, whom these three countries helped put in power by helping get rid of the former dictator Mobutu. Why they tried to assassinate him? Because he thanked them for helping him, paid them and asked them to go back to their country, when their plans were to rule the Congo with Kabila.

Thus, the hypocrisy of the West and America is that they do not point out the truth.

"Security?" Security against whom? The Tutsis' "Security" against the Hutus, or Rwandans' security against other Rwandans?

Why do the so-called world leaders not learn from history? Since independence, back-and-forth, the Tusis and the Hutus have been hunting each other, depending on which group is in power.

So why is America and Europe allowing the innocent Congolese to be killed by the Tutsis of Rwanda, Burundi and Uganda?

It is NOT for security reasons. Because, there are Hutu militias coming from Tanzania who are fighting in Rwanda, in Burundi, and in Uganda. However, Tanzania has not been invaded for "security" reasons, or invaded for the Tutsis to punish or hunt down the Rwandans who participated in the genocide of other Rwandans in 1994. In fact, nobody, not America, not Western Europe, nobody is advancing such a notion, even though there are Hutu refugees in Tanzania.

So, what about the security of these three countries along their borders with Tanzania? Just like what any other country in the world does in these circumstances, these three countries should have their soldiers guarding, from their territories, their borders with Tanzania. International Law dictates that that is all they can do.

But how come this does not apply to the Congo?

As President Clinton would say, "It is the Economy, stupid!"

It is the Congolese resources. It is the diamonds, the gold, the manganese, the silver, the cobalt, the rare minerals, and so on.

And because American and European corporations are the ones helping these three countries steal the Congolese resources, and because American and European corporations are the ones making the most money from these stolen Congolese resources, American and European governments and the media make sure that the truth is not told.

Shame, shame, shame, shame to American and European governments, corporations and the media they control! Shame, shame!

Diamonds, this is the cause for which Congolese women are being buried alive, raped, burned, and killed. And white corporations from America and Europe who are racking in millions from the sale of these diamonds do not care about what is happening to the Congolese women. After all, it is not happening to WHITE women!

Gold, this is the reason why Congolese children are mutilated, killed with machetes, thrown into the bush so that their mothers can be raped by over twenty men at a time. And white corporations in America and Europe, which, not only give weapons to the Rwandans, Ugandans, and

Burundians to slaughter Congolese children, they also own the planes and the industries that bring out and use the Congolese gold, being acquired with the blood of the Congolese children. After all, these are only Black children, not WHITE.

Manganese, Cobalt, silver, and other rare and precious minerals, are the true basis for which the Congolese elderly, the sick, and the invalids are being slaughtered and burned. And the American and European elected heads of states and members of congress or parliament who get the monies for their campaigns from the corporations involved with stealing the Congolese resources are not going to act as forcefully as they did in Kuwait or in Kosovo. After all, it is only Black elderly, Black sick, and Black invalids, not WHITE.

In fact, the true motives behind the invasion of the Congo is so obvious that finally, on April 20th, 2000, *Reuters* reported from the United Nations, in New York, that

*"Secretary-General Kofi Annan has proposed that a panel of experts probe illegal exploitation of the **natural resources of the Democratic Republic of the Congo,** scene of the many-sided conflict."*

But, let us be plain, if the Congolese who are dying were white, neither America, nor Europe was going to wait for the United Nations General-Secretary to "propose" creating a panel to study, debate, write, edit, compromise, and issue declarations or resolutions, while people are being killed every day.

9

The Toll: 1.7 Million Congolese Killed, and Counting...

Reuters, June 9th, 2000, reports from the United Nations, that "1.7 million die in eastern Congo due to war."

This number covers the period of August 1998 through May 2000.

The president of the International Rescue Committee, Reynold Levy, said, comparatively, that

"it is as if the entire population of Houston was wiped off the face of the Earth in a matter of months.

Why are 1.7 million Congolese killed, and the United Nations, the United States, Europe, and everyone else do not forcefully, immediately, without waiting for another Congolese to die, demand that Rwanda, Uganda, and Burundi leave the Congo or make them leave?

These 1.7 million dead Congolese, as a matter of ultimate responsibility, are blamed on President Clinton, in the same way that the 10,000,000-plus Congolese slaughtered under King Leopold II between 1887 and 1908 were blamed on him.

King Leopold II was not only responsible for the overall policy that led to the genocide of the Congolese, but he had, in addition, the ultimate power to stop this genocide if he had wanted to. But he did not. (See Adam Hoschild's *King Leopold's Ghost,* and the upcoming book by this writer titled *Hell in Paradise*)

As for today's Congo, President Clinton is the ultimate person who is making it possible for Rwanda, Burundi, and Uganda to be capable, have the finances, and buy the necessary weapons to carry out this genocide against the Congolese people. Thus, President Clinton has the ultimate power to ORDER Uganda, Rwanda, and Burundi to leave the Congo.

But why is President Clinton not ordering these three countries out of the Congo? As it was said earlier, these are the type of questions we would like to ask the President of the United States of America.

One thing is clear. When Iraq, in the eyes of America, misbehaved, President Clinton did not hesitate to act, and to act swiftly. And, when Serbia moved in Kosovo and started killing the Kosovars, President Clinton did not hesitate to order troops over there to bomb Milosevich's troops out of Kosovo.

Only in Africa, it seems, that America is not ready to move swiftly. It is as if the lives of the Africans are not dear enough as to deserve a swift action from the superpower and its allies.

So, to drag the sufferings of Black Africans, the scheme then is to bring in the United Nations. Because at the UN, conflict resolutions drag on and on for years, which is the reason why America goes it alone when it needs swift resolution of some conflict as in the case of Kosovo, Grenada, Panama, or Haiti.

Because President Clinton is advised by others as to what is going on in the Congo, we hope that the information in this book will help and expose the President to the atrocities being perpetrated in the Congo by Rwanda, Uganda, and Burundi.

10

How Did This Conflict Start? Why is the Truth Not Being Told?

Every time the war in the Congo is written about, the same lies are repeated over and over.

When reporting the crimes, the tortures, the cold-blooded murders committed daily by the Ugandans-Rwandans-Burundians, invariably, even so-called "independent" news-gathering organizations end their stories with a variant of the following quote:

"Uganda, Rwanda and Burundi back various rebel factions fighting the government of President Laurent Kabila, who is backed by troops from Zimbabwe, Angola and Namibia."

The above reads like a football match. It is like a soccer game. It reads or concludes as if there are no bad guys; no violation of the territorial integrity of another country. It sounds like there are no crimes being committed, no atrocities that demand a show of outrage and a strong condemnation of the nations that have invaded another nation.

When one reads these reports, one does not get the truth that the Ugandan-Rwandan-Burundian armies have done something that goes against all international laws and the very charter of the United Nations.

Against the very charter of the United Nations that made the governments and major media of the United States, England, France, and the majority of the UN members daily clamor, denounce, and finally lead a military campaign against Iraq for its invasion of Kuwait.

The way the war in the Congo is reported is as if no one wants to denounce, to offend, to point out that the Ugandans-Rwandans-Ugandans are the murderers, the bad guys, the criminals, the invaders, the ones running a campaign of terror hundreds of miles away from their own borders, deep inside the Congo territory.

This criminal invasion of the Congo is always reported in less accusatory manner.

Some more examples:

"Rwanda has thousands of troops in the Congo and is the driving force behind rebels who took up arms against the Congolese government in 1998."

The "rebels" part is always added as if to legitimize the Rwandans, Ugandans, and Burundians invasion and occupation of the Congo, even though there were no "rebels" when these three countries started the war against the Congo while in the Congo as backers of Kabila.

Another sanitized and non-condemning way is to say that what is happening in the Congo is *"a many-sided conflict in which the government of Congolese President Laurent Kabila (who) is backed by Zimbabwe, Angola and Namibia against the rebel groups and their Rwandan and Ugandan backers."*

The above manner of representing the facts is purposefully intended to keep the reader from expressing outrage about the crimes being committed by the invaders. One does not even get the idea that Rwanda, Uganda, and Burundi are the invaders like Iraq when it invaded Kuwait. That the three countries have NO right, NO excuse to continue to occupy, to continue to murder, to continue to torture and mutilate, to continue to wipe out entire towns of their Congolese populations.

How did this conflict start, what is the truth?

Here is a brief summary of how it started:

As a preamble to the present outright invasion of the Congo by the three armies of Rwanda, Uganda, and Burundi, it should be remembered that the Congo has always been, since the independence of these three countries, a sanctuary of the different lingual groups when persecuted by their fellow countrymen.

In the sixties, these same Tutsis from these three countries, especially those from Rwanda, when the Hutus drove them from power, sought and found refuge in the Congo. Then, in 1994, it was the Hutus' turn to seek refuge when the Tutsis came to power. Back and forth.

What gave these Tutsis the boldness to, this time, invade, occupy, and try to annex a territory or part of it, which is bigger than their own countries?

An analysis and understanding of the situation in the Congo during the waning years of Mobutu's dictatorship can shed some light on this question.

The immediate facts that led to the present situation are as follow:

1. At the beginning of 1994, Rwanda had a government of reconciliation that was made up of both Hutus and Tutsis. The President, Juvenal Abyarimana, was a Hutu. The Head of the Army, Paul Kagame, was a Tutsi.

2. On April 6th, 1994, the plane bringing home President Abyarimana from an overseas trip was shot down, in his own country, and he was killed.

3. The Rwandan Hutus population suspected that the Rwandan Tutsis were responsible for the killing of "their" President. (The United Nations' investigation has, now, concluded that, in fact, Paul Kagame, the Army strongman at the time of Abyarimana's

assassination (and now the president of Rwanda) might have ordered Abyarimana's plane to be shot down.

4. As has been the history of the vengeful and back-and-forth co-genocidal relationship between these two groups, the Hutus started preparing for *revenge.*

5. As everyone knows today, that is exactly what the Hutus did. They took revenge in the 1994 massacre of men, women and children. A massacre that could have been prevented by both the UN and the powers of the world.

6. After this massacre, as the co-genocidal cycle of these three countries goes, the Tutsis got organized and, helped by their lingual brethren in Uganda and Burundi, fought their way back to power. And, as it has been happening before, the Hutus sought refuge in the bordering countries, the Congo (then Zaire) and Tanzania.

7. In 1996-1997, a group called *l'Alliance des Forces Démocratiques pour la Libération du Congo* (AFDL) or the Alliance of the Democratic Forces for the Liberation of the Congo, started a military campaign to remove from power Mobutu Sese Seko, the Zairian dictator who had been ruling Zaire for over 32 years.

8. A Congolese and former follower of Patrice Lumumba by the name of Laurent-Desiré Kabila headed the AFDL. It was backed by and included Ugandan, Rwandan, and Burundian troops:

   • For the Ugandans, they wanted to use this campaign to destroy their fellow Ugandans who belong to a group called "The Lord's Army," who were driven from power in Uganda and now were leading a rebellion campaign from the Zarian territory, from the Sudan and from the Central African Republic.

   • For the Rwandans, meaning the Tutsis who were now in power, they wanted to help in this campaign in order to "hunt down" their fellow Rwandans, the hutus. These were the *Interhamwe* rebels and members of the former Armed Forces of Rwanda and civilians, whether they had participated in the 1994 massacre of the Tutsis or not.

9. This campaign ended up with the AFDL's entrance in Kinshasa on May 17th, 1997, with Mobutu being driven out, and Kabila becoming President of Zaire (later changed to Congo).

10. As a Pan-Africanist, Kabila appointed to positions of power, the Rwandans he thought to be his African brethren who helped in liberating the Congo from Mobutu's dictatorship, asking them to help fix up the chaos that Mobutu created. For example, James KABAREHE, a Rwandan, was appointed Chief of Staff of the Congolese Army. Another Rwandan, Bizima Kahara, was appointed foreign minister in Kabila's government, and so forth.

11. By June 1998, the Congolese people started openly complaining that the Ugando-Rwandan forces that helped Kabila remove Mobutu were not conducting themselves as pan-Africanists, but were rather behaving like occupation forces and were confiscating luxury items, including automobiles, and other goods from the people and flying them back to their home countries.

12. In July 1998, a plot by the Rwando-Ugandans to assassinate Kabila was uncovered, and the next day, the leaders in this plot fled back to Rwanda. On July 29th, 1998, Kabila gave a speech outlining his decision to ask all the outside forces that helped in the liberation of the Congo from dictatorship to return to their own countries. He announced that there would continue to be cooperation, in the African spirit of brotherhood, between these countries and the Congo, in his efforts to re-organize and re-build all the institutions of the state of Congo that had been destroyed by the Mobutu's dictatorship.

13. This decision by Kabila triggered an all out war that was intended to kill Kabila and occupy the Congo (since Rwandan-Burundian-Ugandan forces were all over the Congo, had been helping re-build the Congolese army, and there were no organized and structured Congolese army when they came in with Kabila).

14. A comprehensive plan of occupation of the Congo by Ugandan, Rwandan, and Burundian forces was put into action August 2nd.

15. On the 2nd and 3rd of August, 1998, beside the troops that were stationed already in Kinshasa and all over the Congo, several truckload of Rwandan soldiers with heavy military weapons crossed the border and attacked the Congolese towns of Goma and Bukavu.

16. At the same time, in Kinshasa, thousands of Ugandan and Rwandan soldiers who had helped remove Mobutu, took over the two military bases in Kinshasa, Tshatshi and Kokolo. In the mining town of Kisangani, another Rwando-Ugandan military detachment opened fire and took over the Kisangani military base.

17. On Tuesday, August 4th, 1998, three airplanes with between 600 to 800 Rwandan soldiers, flew from Goma to the military base of Kitona in the Lower Congo province, just over a hundred miles outside of the capital city of Kinshasa.

18. Led by James Kabarehe, the Rwandan who had been entrusted with re-organizing the Congolese army, these multiple operations had the following goals:

    • To rally the former Congolese soldiers under Mobutu to join the Rwandan-Burundian-Ugandan soldiers in their effort to topple the Kabila leadership.
    • To ultimately take over Kinshasa beginning with the sea ports of Matadi, Banana, and Boma on the Atlantic coast.

- To take control of the hydro-electrical dam of Inga, therefore control the electricity that is provided to Kinshasa, the Lower-Congo, and the mining complexes of Katanga, and to several other eastern and central African countries.
- To, then, remove Kabila by either killing him or driving him out of the country by force, and to replace Kabila with a Tutsi regime, or one under Tutsi control.

19.   On Sunday, August 9th, 1998, the Ugandan regular army troops entered the Congo Eastern Province, through Kamango and Watsa, then moved toward the town of Bunia.

20.   On the same day, a Ugandan army transport plane landed in Nebbi, a Ugandan district right across from Mahagi, in Congolese territory. This plane carried weapons that were distributed to the garrisons of Fahidi, Huruti Mbo, and Mee, with the purpose of readying these troops for the ultimate occupation of the Congo.

21.   The Rwandan-Ugandan-Burundian forces actually took over the hydroelectric Inga Dam and they cut off electricity to the Capital city of Kinshasa and the other localities served by the dam.

22.   As they moved towards Kinshasa (and those who were in Kinshasa tried to seize some governmental sites), the people, the Congolese population started fighting back the invaders. With no weapons, the population neutralized the armed Rwandan-Ugandan forces.

23.   From the east to the west, all the way to Kinshasa, the Congo was on the verge of being overrun by the united forces of Rwanda, Uganda and Burundi, former allies and friends. Therefore, the government of the Congo, as a member of

SADC and through its president Laurent Kabila, then, sought help from the other member states in order to defend its territorial integrity and national sovereignty. Zimbabwe, Angola, and Namibia came to the aid of the Congo.

The above is how this conflict started. There were, then, no Congolese "rebels," no "security" concerns for Rwanda, Uganda, or Burundi. These three countries, friends who helped Laurent Kabila remove Mobutu Sese Seko from power, turned against him when he asked them to leave. Then, in order to legitimize their campaign against the Congo, they set up the so-called rebels as a front to cover their deeds.

In fact, quoting their governments' officials, the Western media news reports in 1997, after Kabila and his allies at the time (Rwanda, Uganda, and Burundi) took power in the Congo, were that Kabila and his allies "were killing the Hutus refugees" who had run into the Congo after the 1994 Rwandan genocide. No "rebels!" No "security concerns!"

11

The Congolese Religious Faiths' Statement of Solidarity and Protest

Since August 2nd, 1998, the Democratic Republic of the Congo is fighting a war of aggression-rebellion, which all of us deplore. This war has brought about other wars: an increase in the cost of living, a constant hiking of commodities' prices, a downward value of the currency, a deterioration of the economic fabric of the country, gasoline shortages, almost non-existent public transportation, degradation of social conditions, destruction of national infrastructures such as schools, hospitals, and roads, the cancellation of the vaccination campaign in the occupied territories, etc. In brief, the ever worsening social misery have reached a level that no human being can stand.

As if the deaths and sufferings caused by this war were not enough, the latest developments are so shocking that we must energetically raise our voice again in protest.

A few days ago, the two invading armies of Rwanda and Uganda, fighting in Kisangani over our resources that they have been stealing, killed several innocent people in this Congolese diamond city, which is the capital of the Eastern Province.

These two foreign armies are fighting each other in our country. What a violation of international law! And this, without any immediate and concrete action on the part of the international community, the United Nations, the European Union, or the OAU! What humiliation for the Congolese army! What humiliation for an entire people!

TO THE INTERNATIONAL COMMUNITY

Taking into account our pastoral responsibility before God, before the people, and being witnesses of the events taking place in our country, we, the leaders of the Catholic, Protestant, Orthodox, Kimbanguist, and Islamic faiths in Kinshasa,

- *Forcefully condemn the stealing of our resources and the merciless killing of our people by the foreign armies in our country, especially those of Rwanda and Uganda, who will one day leave us with a ruined, looted, and exsanguine exploited country.*
- *Demand that the international community, especially the great powers, use all their influence in order to immediately put a stop to this war that continues to slaughter our people, who have already been weakened by all these elements. We demand that the international community, especially the major powers, insure the immediate implementation of the Lusaka Accords.*
- *Denounce the strategies of the weapons manufacturers who provoke and maintain these wars in order to keep selling their merchandise.*
- *Call on the African heads of States to avoid all armed conflicts and all actions that are destructive to their own people.*
- *Recall the idea of African Unity that drove the fathers of African independence, and the promotion of African culture, of tolerance, of reconciliation, and of peace.*

- *Request that the religious faiths in the countries that have invaded our nation publicly condemn the acts of their governments and ask them to withdraw their armies, and respect the territorial integrity of the Democratic Republic of the Congo.*

TO THE CONGOLESE NATION

Taking into account our pastoral responsibility before God, before the people, and being witnesses of the events taking place in our country, we, the leaders of the Catholic, Protestant, Orthodox, Kimbanguist, and Islamic faiths in Kinshasa,

- *Equally invite the Head of State LAURENT DESIRE KABILA, to relax the political space of the Democratic Republic of the Congo.*
- *Also invite the sons and daughters of our beloved Congo to work together for our national reconstruction and dialogue in order to undertake the rebuilding of our nation as we enter the new Millennium.*
- *Express our condolences to our brothers and sisters who have lost family members during this war, and we salute the memory of our fallen martyrs and, particularly those killed in Kisangani.*

United in our faith in God, master of life and of history, we encourage you, brothers and sisters, to always count on God's love for his people, especially in this moment of great trials in our country. Remember that God never abandons his people.

May the God of peace keep us all in His love, and may He protect the Democratic Republic of the Congo.

Kinshasa, August 23rd, 1999.

(Signed):
For the Catholics,
Cardinal FREDERIC ETSHOU NZABI BAMUNGWABI

For the Protestants,
Mgr. PIERRE MARINI BODHO,
National President of the Church of Christ in the Congo.

For the Orthodoxy,
Father Reverend DAVID KATALAYI,
Secretary of the Archdiocese of Central Africa.

For the Muslims,
EL HADJ MUDILO WA MALEMBA

Epilogue

This world is led by those who have the power to impose their will. As the African saying goes, the lion is always right and his will always prevails over that of the antelope.

The difference between animals and humans is that humans are supposed to be able to sit down together and decide on who is right and who is wrong when two parties are in dispute. Unfortunately, humans, as in the case of the war in the Congo, can be even more unjust, more cunning, more brutal, more cold-blooded than the worst animal carnivores.

The genocide in the Congo continues, as of this June, 2000.

The reports coming out of Kisangani are confirming the killing of 600 Congolese civilians during the fighting between the Rwandan and the Ugandan soldiers.

Anyone who can look at a map and see where Kisangani is in relation to the borders of either Rwanda or Uganda and say that these two countries are justified to be that deep inside the Congo, fight over a town that belong to neither one, and continue to kill innocent people, anyone who will justify this or not demand that these two countries go back to their own countries, is a murderer and a criminal just like these killers.

In fact, it can be safely said that, the Rwandans, the Ugandans, the Burundians, and all those who are supporting and defending their illegal invasion and occupation of the Congo are going to be held accountable, sooner or later.

The international community refuses to come out strongly to condemn and take decisive action to protect the innocent people of the Congo. Because, it is said, the European and the American governments "like" Museveni, the president of Uganda, and Kagame and the Tutsis of Rwanda.

So, the innocent lives of Congolese women, children, the elderly and the handicapped matter little or not at all?

For all these insane, cold-blooded reasons, the world community stalls, hiding behind the United Nations, especially the powerful nations.

More horror tales keep coming out of the Congo:

The invading forces of Rwanda, Uganda and Burundi, those occupying and operating in the Northeast of the Congo, massacred 281 civilians, cutting their heads off.

According to the news agency *Reuters*, June 13, 2000:

"In the Bomongo sector, no later than this morning, we discovered more than 238 headless bodies of civilians in piles. We also found 43 bodies among the small islands in the Nkiri River."

And, while the killing of the innocent Congolese women, children, the elderly, and the disabled continues,

- **WESTERN EUROPE:** the so-called *Paris Club*, the group of European countries that give money to the invaders of the Congo, conduct themselves as if there is nothing wrong with the atrocities that these three countries have been committing: *"Western governments argue that as long as Uganda keeps defence expenditure to within two percent of gross domestic product (GDP) they* **will turn A BLIND EYE TO THE COUNTRY'S INVOLVEMENT IN THE CONGO, where it is thought to have more than 10,000 troops supporting two rebel** *groups."* Kampala, Uganda, June 13th, 2000 (Reuters). In other words, as long as Uganda is killing the Congolese mothers and children using only 2% of the money, Europe would continue to fund this enterprise. Europe won't lift a finger to stop this horror, this genocide.

• **AMERICA:** The United States Government has no qualm with Rwanda's campaign of genocide in the Congo: *"Rwanda Gets **World Bank Loans** Even as UN Condemns Congo Fighting."* Washington, D.C., June 7th, 2000 (Bloomberg). The same American government, the same President Clinton who stood in East Africa and said that America should have done something to stop the killing of 800,000 Rwandans by their fellow Rwandans, is sitting back, giving money to, and not stopping the Rwandans from killing 1.7 million Congolese.

• **RUSSIA:** yes, Russia also is involved on the side of those decimating the Congolese people: *"At least 21 people including five Rwanda army officers were killed when a transport plane crashed in the east of the Democratic Republic of the Congo. A Russian-built Antonov-8...crashed between five and eight minutes after take-off...The five officers had been on their way to Kigali for the swearing-in ceremony on Saturday of Rwanda's newly named president, Paul Kagame...The nationalities of the other 15...had probably included Rwandans, Congolese and perhaps **a Russian crew.**"* Kigali, Rwanda, April 20, 2000 (Reuters).

Why are European and American governments so insensitive to the deaths of Congolese?

How come, when white Europeans or Americans are killed, European and American governments take UNILATERAL and immediate action to put a stop to it, but when Blacks or third world people are killed, American and European governments drag their feet, hide behind the unending debates and resolutions of the UN, while American and European gun-makers bring more weapons in these countries, killing more and more people?

How many more million Congolese do Rwandan, Ugandan, and Burundian armies have to slaughter, with European and American weapons bought with American and European monies, and transported by Russians with Russian airplanes?

Please, write, call, e-mail, fax to your president, as well as your elected officials, and tell them to pressure the head of your government to take all immediate actions in their power and put a stop to the genocide in the Congo. Now! Today! Immediately!

Only your voice, only the voices of the hundreds, the thousands, the millions, when heard, can overpower the millions of dollars that are given to the heads of your governments and your elected officials to buy their silence, and for them to look the other way. Millions and millions of dollars are made from diamonds, gold, silver, manganese, cobalt, and dozens of rare minerals from the Congo. Millions of dollars that are costing the lives, the mutilations, the starvation, the misery of millions of Congolese women, children, the elderly, the handicapped, and their men.

About the Author

Professor Yaa-Lengi Ngemi (Malcolm-King College, The College of New Rochelle) is a native of the Democratic Republic of the Congo (ex-Zaire) in Central Africa. He is the Official Translator, from French into English, of Cheikh Anta Diop's much heralded book, **Civilization or Barbarism** and the author of **The Study Guide to Civilization or Barbarism**. Professor Ngemi just completed his book on the Congo titled, **Hell in Paradise** (which documents the genocide, mutilations, slavery, and rape in the Congo, 1884-1960).

A multi-dimensional scholar, Professor Ngemi has lectured at colleges, universities (both in Africa and in the US), community forums, and other venues including Queens College, Fairleigh Dickinson University, Rutgers University, Temple University, The University of Medicine and Dentistry of New Jersey, Borough of Manhattan Community College, Queens Borough Langston Hughes Community Library and Cultural Center, New York City Public Library Harlem Branch, ATT-Bell Laboratories, The African-American Museum of Hempstead, L.I., The United Nations,...He has also been a guest on Cable and Public television shows (i.e., The Tony Brown Journal, The Melanin Chronicles...) and radio programs.

Professor Ngemi holds undergraduate and graduate degrees in business administration, history, education, and the sciences from The Salvation

Army College in Kinshasa, Congo, from Louisiana State University and Southern University in Baton Rouge, Louisiana, and from Columbia University in New York, New York. He has taught the sciences (Biology, Environmental Science and Chemistry), Math, and African History on the college level, and Physics, Chemistry, Biology, Math, French and English on the junior high and high school levels.

Prof. Ngemi is the Director of Research *of the New York-based African Research and Educational Institute, Inc., a not-for-profit institution.*

While teaching at the College of New Rochelle and translating Diop's book in The Black Studies Department of the City College (City University of New York), he developed a six-credit course on the African Contribution to Humanity in the Sciences, The Humanities, and the Arts, based on Civilization or Barbarism *and other sources. He, later, simplified this course and has been teaching it at the community level as a twenty-two hour course titled "Africa-World 2001, Initiation Into Original Knowledge," using* Civilization or Barbarism *and other sources.*

[Due to numerous demands from all over the United States after his appearance on "The Tony Brown Journal", Professor Ngemi has been conducting intensive, 3-day week-end study of this book in the different regions of the U.S.]

The author can be reached at 212-690-1851, E-mail: *theafricanresearch.ei@netzero.net or yaalengimn@aol.com*; or write to P.O. Box 7309, New York, NY 10116 (USA).

Three Appendixes

The following three appendixes are articles written by the author at different times in the recent history of the Congo, beginning with the removal of Mobutu by Kabila and his forces in 1997. All three articles were published in the New York City daily newspaper, *THE DAILY CHALLENGE.*

The author visited the Congo a month and-a-half after Kabila took over. What the author witnessed, after 20 years of absence, is reported in *Appendix 1.*

In 1998, when Rwanda, Uganda, and Burundi attempted to assassinate Kabila and take over power in the Congo, the author wrote an article on what went on and what was its significance. This is *Appendix 2.*

Appendix 3 is an open letter to the United States Ambassador to the United Nations, Richard Holbrooke, published on the day that the said ambassador convened a special meeting at the United Nations to talk about the conflict in the Congo.

The three appendixes are published here so that the reader understands the context within which the genocide in the Congo is taking place. We believe that the reader is intelligent enough to understand the kind of hypocrisy being displayed by the powers supporting Uganda, Rwanda, and Burundi's invasion and occupation of another country, the Congo (Zaire).

Appendix 1

Mobutu's Hell, Kabila's Hope

A native son returns to former Zaire as eyewitness to new Congo
(PART I)
(*Daily Challenge*, Wednesday, October 8, 1997, page 8)
By Prof. Yaa-Lengi Ngemi

On May 27, 1997, Kabila's AFDL (Alliance of the Forces of Liberation)—comprised of mostly young fighters—entered Kinshasa, the capital city of Zaire, now renamed Congo, with Mobutu fleeing the huge country that he had sworn he would never leave to become an ex-president. This date marked the end of Mobutu's 32 years of the most shameful dictatorship in the entire modern history of Africa.

On July 18, 1997, just over a month later, I set foot on my native country's soil after a total absence of 21 years (save for a few days spent in Kinshasa 12 years ago on my way back to the US from visiting my parents in the interior).

Now, who said that Black Africans could not run a country void of corruption? Landing at the International Ndjili Airport in Kinshasa, I was so proud to experience an orderly entry into the country without hassle or request for bribery. What a pleasure to enter into one's native country in such a civilized way.

Frequent visitors to Kinshasa breathed an air of relief that the phalanxes of Mobutu's tribal members, even those who could not read or write, were no longer at the airport grabbing passengers, confiscating whatever goods they wanted out of their luggage and, in addition, requiring them to pay for their entry into the country whether their passports were in order or not.

Oh, but what chaos, what destruction, what dilapidation, what misery of all sorts did I see as I rode with my family from the airport across the city all the way to the commune (district) of Bandalungwa Bisengo, almost at the other end of this burgeoning but decayed city of six million souls. (Nobody really knows the exact count).

The only conclusion that I could come up with was that Mobutu not only copied well King Leopold II in his genocidal policies which he used on his own people, he, by far, out-did Leopold II in the fact that he made the people suffer and die just because they had rejected him and had dared to ask for justice and democracy and the right to choose who would lead them.

The things I saw and heard as my big brother Maseke's four-by-four dual cabin small pick up truck bounced and screamed through holes that could swallow a V8 Cadillac, made tears come to my eyes.

In the first place, almost everybody, including the members of my family, looked like they were dying from a long sickness that has prevented them from taking in food. I found out that they were in "good" health, except that malnutrition and, for most people, zero-nutrition is the cause of most of them looking like padded-up skeletons. Why? Not only did Mobutu drive the country into deflation, but he made sure that the infrastructure (roads) decayed so that a trip that used to take half-a-day in a 4x4 now takes one whole week (forget using a car or a regular pick up truck to travel into the interior, you might end up abandoning it in some ravine or sinking mud, broken beyond repair). Then, Mobutu put his forces at all entrances into the city for them to seize all the foodstuff coming into the city and destroy it so that people would not have anything to eat.

As a result, parents turned some city roads into fields, yes, growing vegetables on what used to be cemented city roads just so that they can have something to feed the children. And the children, oh, the children! I could not hold back tears to see children going two days without a meal, or a mother holding her baby on the side of the street, both skeleton-looking, begging for something to eat or for money. Young people and adults were selling drinking water in small plastic bags. People sold the shirts on their back—or anything else they could find—so that they could buy even salted fish scales to cook with vegetables and give it a taste of fish. Mothers at the *market, picking up from the ground (dirt) grains of rice or corn, one by one, so that they could gather a handful to go feed the children. The sick dying without treatment. Students, not only going to school hungry (one must be wealthy to eat any meal before night time or to afford two meals a day) but they and their parents, most of whom are jobless or unpaid, must come up with the money to pay the teachers and the university professors before they can teach. They must pay to take tests or to get their results.*

To top this, in order for one to get a job in Mobutu's government, in any position, one had to swear to do evil to the people. Even a private business person could not fix a road or any public structure without being warned that one would lose one's business or one's life.

Then there was the physical terrorizing of the people, the cold-blooded killings, the organized bands that ransacked people's homes at night, killing, maiming and raping; and when one was thought of having resisted or challenged anyone under Mobutu's people's protection (including all of the foreign merchants), a band of armed people would break into one's home at night and do whatever they planned.

A story is told of a man who resisted a Mobutu's protégé who had decided to take away the man's wife. They broke into his house at night, woke up everybody, and with the entire family watching, told his first son to have sex with his mother right there or both he and his father would be killed. Both father and son chose death and were shot dead as the wife and the other children watched.

Sometimes the greed reached the ridiculous, such as the case of one of Mobutu's sisters who, while watching TV one night, liked the TV male host, so she called her brother, Mobutu, and told him about it. Mobutu picked up the phone and ordered the man to come lunch at his house. When the man came, he was told that he had to leave his wife and children and become Mobutu's sister's husband, and that he, Mobutu, was going to pay money to the man's family. Mobutu further stipulated that the man could never seek to even see his wife or visit his children.

The horror stories go on and on.

Mobutu's undercover and uniformed forces fed off the people. Even during the daytime, they could stop you and confiscate your car. If they liked what you had on, they ordered you (in front of everybody, and you knew that they would shoot you right there if you resisted) to undress and whatever they wanted became theirs. By the way, if Mobutu's people liked your house, they took it away from you, too. Law and order no longer existed. In order to survive, one had to know somebody in Mobutu's government or army.

Oh yes, in the middle of all of this, diamonds, gold, and other minerals were still flowing out of Zaire. A tiny minority ate well, lived good lives, drove expensive automobiles and slept in expensive houses—especially if they associated themselves with anyone connected to Mobutu. And where did all the money in the country go? Well, beside the billions that Mobutu stole and the West allowed him to hide in their countries, whatever was left in the country was freely taken by those who served Mobutu.

Among the many sad and criminal cases is the case of one army colonel who went to a local bank in Kinshasa and asked for money. The bank clerk asked him to present a check or give his account number so that they could help him withdraw money from his account. He said he did not have an account there, but he needed money. They told him they could not just give him money like that. So the colonel picked up his cellular phone and called Mobutu who then asked to speak to the bank president, and ordered him to give the colonel as much money as he wanted.

One of Mobutu's ministers had 200 houses to himself. Another one had a huge yard in Kinshasa where he kept 75 luxury automobiles from around the world so that he could drive a different car in the morning, in the afternoon and at night. Another head of a government agency in Kinshasa gave himself a $40,000 salary, plus a $5,000 weekly bonus, took ownership of all of the government agency's buildings then rented them back to the agency. He then told Mobutu that it was not good for people to always come bother the president of the country for help and that if anyone asked for help, for Mobutu to send them to him. Mobutu praised this guy who, then, would

confiscate or cut the workers' salary as he pleased to give it to the people
that Mobutu sent to him.

(Tomorrow, Part II: Enter KABILA)

Mobutu's Hell, Kabila's Hope

A native son returns to former Zaire as eyewitness to new Congo
(PART II)

(*Daily Challenge*, Thursday, October 9, 1997, page 5)

By Prof. Yaa-Lengi Ngemi

Enter Kabila!

In barely a month after Mobutu's flight and fleeing, the terrorizing of
the people and the criminal acts against them have stopped. For sure, there
are still small bands of the criminals who operated under Mobutu who still
go out at night to terrorize and steal form the people, but Kabila's forces
stay vigorously on their heels, and when these elements are caught, they
dearly pay and the people rejoice. As a result, the Congolese people have
hope.

The people, on their own, are fixing even the roads in front of their
houses (which was "illegal" to do during Mobutu's dictatorship).

When one speaks with the people on the streets, in the mini buses or
taxis—whether they speak Lingala, Kituba, Swahili or Tshiluba—they tell
you they are thankful to God and the ancestors who heard their cries and
their prayers and allowed Kabila to come and remove Mobutu. They
know—oh yes, they know and would tell anyone who would listen—that
America and Europe put Mobutu there and kept him there, and that
nobody cared about their plight enough to remove Mobutu. All the West
cared about, people say, was the wealth, the resources of the country, which
Mobutu gave to them for relative pittances. Of course, one cannot expect a

mother whose child is dying of malnutrition in her hands to understand the intricacies of international diplomacy.

True, there is still hunger. Curable diseases are still killing the people. The infrastructure is still dilapidated. But I saw and felt the signs of renewal, beginning at Ndjili International Airport.

Kabila, more than anyone else, understands that it is going to take everybody's effort to rebuild this huge country that has been called the wealthiest in Africa in natural resources, but one that Mobutu turned into the poorest in the world.

In a bid to address these conditions, Kabila invited native intellectuals from all over the world to come back and help rebuild the country. And, to make things easy, his government pays for their hotel accommodations and food as they go out and apply for positions related to their expertise or training.

It took Mobutu 32 years to destroy the country and the people's bodies, souls, and spirits. How anyone expects Kabila to change things in less than six months is beyond common sense and comprehension. Indeed, there is talk here overseas that Kabila is not allowing the "opposition" to speak out. Cow dung! I went, I saw, and I heard! And, lest anyone accuses me of partisanship, not only do I not belong to Kabila's tribe or lingual group, but I have been the elected president and representative in New York City of the largest opposition group to Mobutu, the UDPS, and my party was founded on the principles of the struggle for Democracy in Zaire (now Congo).

While in Kinshasa, in the daily newspapers, I read the criticisms of Kabila, his government or appointees. I was there when a large group of the PALU political party members marched. No one stopped them until they got to the end of their march when, whatever caused it, an AFDL soldier fired and killed three people. The soldier was arrested.

These are isolated cases in a country and a city that, no more than three months ago, lived under the most heinous regime that, at any given *hour, committed the most unbelievable criminal acts and carnage against the people.*

My party fought for Mobutu to go and for democracy to come. Mobutu was removed by force following warfare, not a coup or through negotiations or elections.

The largest majority of the people in the Congo understand, and most of the other political parties—as well as the majority of the UDPS leadership—understand that Kabila has asked, and we must join him to, first, re-establish the country's basic structures and infrastructure before, as Kabila has promised, convening a referendum on a new and permanent and democratic constitution before elections are held.

Isn't this the proper thing to do?

Now the West, the very cause of Mobutu's existence, is threatening to not help the Congo and Kabila's government because he is resisting the investigation of the killings of some Rwandan refugees in Zaire during Kabila's war to get Mobutu and his criminal government out.

Why? Why?

Does the West really care about those refugees? Where was the West when a quarter-of-a million of Tutsis were murdered by their brothers Hutus in 1994 so that, today, you are going to investigate if the Tutsis who were fighting along with Kabila killed some of their fellow Hutus during the war?

Has the West investigated itself about the guilty or the innocent people that died during the wars the West has fought? Or is it that Kabila is disliked because he might be genuinely interested in uplifting his people, and, therefore, they don't want to help him succeed?

Fortunately, this kind of sick thinking does not come from the American people or from the general population in the West, but from some policymakers who have other things in mind when they are talking like this. These are the same people who helped and paid for Mobutu to get Lumumba killed, looked the other way while Mobutu stole billions of dollars and killed his own people, deprived them of food, health care, and education while destroying even the environment and the natural beauty of his country.

So, from Mobutu's hell to the hope that Kabila has brought to his people and country, the need is for all the people and governments of goodwill around the world (even the UN) to help the Congo and its people rebuild what Mobutu and his 32 years of murderous dictatorship had destroyed.

Appendix 2

Independent Black Africa Coming of Age?

Meaning of the Coalition Supporting Laurent Kabila and the Congo
(*Daily Challenge Weekend Edition*, August 28-30, 1998, page 5)
By Professor Yaa-Lengi Ngemi

In the first week of the present attempt to overthrow the Kabila govern-ment, the US and France closed their embassies in Kinshasa. Here in the West, the media did not give Kabila a chance and no one advocated com-ing to the aid of his government. If anything, those who wanted to over-throw Kabila were interviewed and quoted profusely.

Nobody sought out Kabila or the Congolese people's views.

In early 1960's when Patrice Lumumba was assassinated by the West (CIA and Western Europe) only one African country tried to help the Lumumba's government: Nkwame Nkrumah's Ghana. The West, while secretly setting up Mobutu and undermining Lumumba, was sending sol-diers in and around the Congo only for the purpose of "evacuating their citizens." After Lumumba was killed, the US and Western Europe set Mobutu as the tool, agent, and conduit to be used to try to prevent Zimbabwe (the former Rhodesia), Angola, Mozambique, and Namibia from becoming independent, and South Africa from abolishing Apartheid. Like today, the US and the West did not care about the people of the Congo or of southern Africa, as long as the West's interests were neither threatened nor jeopardized.

Today, Angola, Zimbabwe, Namibia, Mozambique are independent, and physical Apartheid has been abolished.

Today, Zimbabwe and Angola, as independent Black nations that remember recent history, have joined forces to help the Kabila government and the Congolese people. They have done this because they know what Kabila has meant for the Congolese people while here, in the West, nobody talks about the connection between Kabila and the ending of the plight that the Congolese people suffered during the 32 years of the worst dictatorship in recent memory (see Daily Challenge of 10/8 and 10/9, 1997).

What needs to be understood—what Black people in the Diaspora need to understand—is that the West has not yet begun to treat Black African nations as truly independent, and Black Africans as their equals. The interests of the West come before the African people's interests, and, to achieve this, Black stooges are used against both their own people and against other Africans. It is, therefore, imperative that Black people do not rush to always acquiesce with the views given in the media in the West (save CNN, which often times present the news, not biased views) when it comes to Black Africa.

Western media has not told the true story of what has been going on in the Congo. Do the Congolese people want the Rwandan, Ugandan and Mobutu's former soldiers to rule over them? Why did the Congolese people's view of the Rwandans change, leading Kabila to ask them to leave— these same Rwandans and Ugandans who were welcomed by the Congolese as true African brothers for helping Kabila liberate them from Mobutu's dictatorship?

As for the reason given by the enemy of Africa and of the Congolese people that Rwanda would want to occupy the Congo (which is 100 times larger than Rwanda) or part of it for security concerns, those with intelligence should remember that the Hutus and the Tutsis did not start killing each other last year when Kabila took over in the Congo. This co-genocide has been going on for more than a hundred years since the Belgians convinced one group of Rwandans that they were better than the other, and they became so brainwashed that they believed it too.

The sad part is that even after independence, as a nation, Rwandans has not realized that Belgium's policy was intended to divide in order to conquer them and that both Hutus and the Tutsis are Black people who must share this small piece of real-estate called Rwanda.

The solution to Rwandan security, therefore, resides in both lingual groups sitting down under the African Ancestral Tree of Dialogue, acknowledging and extirpating from their souls the enemy of division that the Belgians put in, credit all the past co-killings to Belgium, then sincerely agree to live together as Black African brothers and sisters.

Now, if the Blacks in South Africa can agree to live in peace with the descendants of the non-African whites who treated them worse than animals during Apartheid, then Hutus and Tutsis who are both Black and original Africans, should be able to wake up from the coma of caucasoid brainwashing and division and agree to live together as brothers and sisters.

Black Africa is coming of age and maturing, and the Congolese people are today thankful for it. They are thankful to their brothers and sisters from Angola, Zimbabwe and elsewhere who are coming to their aid while America and Western Europe take flight and conspire. Now, Black Africa needs to heighten its vigilance so that today's Black African leaders who love their people do not meet the same fate at the hands of the West as Patrice Lumumba and Nkwame Nkrumah did.

Appendix 3

A Message to Ambassador Richard Holbrooke:

We Africans Are No Fools!
(Daily Challenge Monday, January 24, 2000, pages 2-3)
By Professor Yaa-Lengi Ngemi

The meeting you are convening at the UN on Jan. 24, 2000 on the issue of the war in the Congo/Zaire, from a historical standpoint, is a humongous farce and a stupendous insult.

Nevertheless, our always-trusting Black African leaders—those who know and those who are ignorant of the lessons of history—are going to attend because Superpower America is calling, and with the hope that America will, this time, do the right thing.

But, what is "the truth," Ambassador Holbrooke? What is the historical truth?

The Historical Truth is, grosso modo, that there would not be a war today in the eastern part of the Congo (or for that matter, anywhere else in Africa) if there were no minerals in those regions.

Who is mining and selling the minerals in the area occupied by the outside forces (Rwanda/Burundi/Uganda) while the war is going on in the Congo?

You, Ambassador must really think of Africans as the stupidest beings on earth who cannot see or say what is really going on!

Rwanda and Uganda invaded the Congo in 1998 after President Kabila refused to just give away the minerals of the Congo to Western corporations as the dictator-criminal Mobutu Sese Seko did for 32 years. How come, Ambassador Holbrooke, we do not hear this out of your mouth?

You really must think of Africans as the most scared beings on earth who cannot tell you in your face what countries and what corporations are reaping monies from the sale of these minerals and financing a war that is

*killing, maiming, and starving men, women, and children while you use
the UN to shield these forces! And that is the real issue here.*

*America and Europe (the Paris Club) support Uganda militarily and
economically, and in addition, The World Bank, IMF, and Uganda support Rwanda and Burundi. These three countries invaded the Congo, and,
according to Reuters (12/1/99), now have white American mercenaries
fighting alongside them in the Congo.*

*How then dare you, Ambassador Holbrooke, pretend like America has
not taken sides in the Congo? You really must believe that Africans are the
dumbest beings on earth who cannot even spell the name of the superpower behind these African stooges who are being used to continue the
killing, maiming, and raping of Africans and their resources!*

*When Kuwait was invaded, America went in and kicked out the
invaders. When Kosovo was invaded, America went in and kicked out the
invaders. Why then, Ambassador Holbrooke, are you convening a meeting
at the United Nations when it comes to an African country that has been
invaded? Do you think that Africans are not aware that America used the
United Nations in 1960-61 to destabilize the Congo and to get the only
democratically elected leader of that country, Patrice Lumumba, assassinated; and that it was America that, not only installed and kept the dictator Mobutu in power for 32 years, but it is again America who, today, is
supporting Uganda, Rwanda, and Burundi against the Congo?*

*You really must be convinced that Africans are the biggest fools on earth
who do not even remember their own recent history and the real power
behind their misery!*

*In 1998, before Uganda, Rwanda, and Burundi, in their war against the
Congo, brought in former Mobutu servants and associates and touted
them as "rebels," the corporate mouthpieces in the West, both in government and in the media never mentioned the word "rebels" who did not
exist then. These media were screaming that the three countries were in the
Congo only to protect and secure Rwanda's border which, by the way, is so
tiny (Rwanda being 100 times smaller than the Congo) that 1000 soldiers*

*can monitor that border without any one passing through undetected. How come, Ambassador Holbrooke, no one is talking about protecting Rwanda's borders anymore, which can be achieved by stationing the UN troops **along** the border between the Congo and Rwanda and Uganda but **never** inside independent and sovereign Congo? How come no one is telling the truth that these internal conflicts in Rwanda are also happening in Burundi and in Uganda where different tribes (Hutus/Tutsis) are using European and American weapons to kill their own people; and that no Congolese ever tried to invade either one of these, but that, on the contrary, the Congo has offered hospitality to these tribes at different times when they were running away from their fellow countrymen?*

You really must believe, as you look at us, that Africans have no brains like yours so that they cannot even think out a simple proposition like "one country invading and occupying another country," or "African minerals acquired cheaply enrich some Americans and Europeans while Africans linger in poverty and sheer misery!"

Finally, those of us who believe in the American creed and its ideals often times must face and denounce the American government's hypocrisy, which puts it, especially concerning Africa, almost always on the side of Africa's tyrants, Africa's oppression, and Africa's misery. Only the actions of the American people in support of Africa's freedom and well being, and their protests against the misdeeds of the American government and some corporations in Africa help Africans see past these crimes in order to appreciate and emulate America's ideals.

Would the Clinton Administration end its term on the side of peace and justice in, and safeguard the sovereignty and territorial integrity of the Congo/Zaire? Or would it follow in the footsteps of those previous American administrations that have helped maintain the Congo, from its inceptions, in a constant state of misery and poverty: from condoning and participating (through US corporations) in the crimes of King Leopold II, to the killing of Patrice Lumumba? From the setting up of the criminal Mobutu, to the attempt now to break up the Congo (so that America and

Europe can control Congo's minerals) and get rid of Kabila using Uganda, Rwanda, and Burundi?

With all due respect, Ambassador Holbrooke, you are not crazy enough to think that Africans are so dumb and crazy that they are going to conduct themselves like enslaved people who are still in chains and who are going to willingly accept the evil, the violence, the rape done to them, their people, their land, their resources, and their humanity, without a protest or a fight, are you?

★★★

37005947R00071

Made in the USA
Lexington, KY
14 November 2014